STRATEGIES TO BUILD WOMEN LEADERS GLOBALLY

STRATEGIES TO BUILD WOMEN LEADERS GLOBALLY

Think Managers, Think Men; Think Leaders, Think Women

PROFESSOR M.S. RAO

FOREWORD BY
M. VENKAIAH NAIDU
VICE-PRESIDENT OF INDIA

Waterside Publishing

Printed in the United States of America

First Printing, 2019

ISBN-13: 978-1-949003-10-9 print edition
ISBN-13: 978-1-939116-13-0 eBook edition

 Waterside Publishing

2055 Oxford Ave
Cardiff, CA 92007
www.waterside.com

TABLE OF CONTENTS

ENDORSEMENTS

International Acclaim for Professor M.S. Rao's Book!

"I extend my greetings and congratulations to Professor M.S. Rao, for his book "Strategies to Build Women Leaders Globally: Think Managers, Think Men; Think Leaders, Think Women." Dedicated to great personalities namely Rosa Parks, Maya Angelou and Oprah Winfrey and issues associated with the empowerment of women, I hope this book will provide a number of insights that will inspire many readers. I congratulate Professor M.S. Rao."

M. Venkaiah Naidu,
Vice-President of India

"Professor M.S. Rao advocates gender equality globally. In this book, he describes the most critical challenges women leaders face today and offers proven techniques for meeting them! The case studies and expert analysis in this book will elevate your leadership and leverage motivational power in your organization!"

Marshall Goldsmith
A Thinkers 50 Top Ten Global Business Thinker
and top ranked executive coach.

"A colleague taught me that women are the largest growth market in the world today (more than China, India,

Indonesia, or Brazil). Professor M.S. Rao's new book offers exceptional insights into this established and emerging global market. His advice will help women at any level, in any organization, and in any country become more competent leaders while not losing their uniqueness."

Dave Ulrich
Rensis Likert Professor, Ross School of
Business, University of Michigan
Partner, the RBL Group

"Professor M.S. Rao's new book advocates servant leadership and gender equality globally. It illustrates with inspiring examples of women leaders including Melinda Gates, Michelle Obama, Angela Merkel, Indra Nooyi, Ursula Burns, and Meg Whitman. Reading this book will broaden your view of how servant leadership can deliver a leadership style that increases engagement and builds trust."

Garry Ridge,
President & CEO WD-40 Company

"Professor MS Rao, the Father of Soft Leadership, has long focused on identifying and developing talent. In this important new book, Professor Rao presents strategies to cultivate perhaps the greatest underutilized resource in our midst: female leadership. Any individual or enterprise will find much that is informative, stimulating and actionable in this hands-on manual from a longtime international leadership guru."

James Strock,
author, Serve to Lead

"Professor M.S. Rao's vision is to develop one million students into global leaders by 2030. *Strategies to Build Women Leaders Globally* provides a compelling argument that women are not only entitled to equal opportunity, but that they are also extremely well suited to become CEOs. This book provides a roadmap, supplemented with tools and techniques, to help women achieve their true potential. In his typical fashion, Professor Rao offers great insight and practical wisdom. I highly recommend it."

Frank Sonnenberg
Award-winning author of seven books, including
Managing with a Conscience and Soul Food:
Change Your Thinking, Change Your Life

"An inspiring guide for the rise of women everywhere! A manifesto for awakening females! I loved it!"

Dr. Joe Vitale
Author Zero Limits and The Awakening Course

"This work by Professor M.S. Rao comes at a pivotal time in history. Women are demanding their equal share in the workplace and in society. Gender equity is at the forefront of almost every conversation. Professor M.S. Rao as always has his finger on the pulse of the issue and developed a work that is needed as well as timely. Kudos Professor M.S. Rao."

Dr. Terry Jackson
Marshall Goldsmith 100 Coach
COO Jackson Consulting Group
Best Selling Author

"International Leadership Guru, Professor M.S. Rao, Ph.D. advocates gender equality globally (#HeForShe). In his book 'Strategies to Build Women Leaders Globally', he illustrates with inspiring examples of women leaders including Melinda Gates, Michelle Obama, Hillary Clinton, Angela Merkel, Indra Nooyi, Ursula Burns, Meg Whitman, and Sheryl Sandberg. He inspires women to smash through the glass ceiling to achieve gender equality globally. I highly recommend this book for a deserved place on your leadership bookshelf."

Dr. Kiran Bedi
IPS (Retd), Author, Lieutenant Governor of
Puducherry. IIT Delhi Alumni, Nehru Fellow,
Magsaysay Awardee, Asian Tennis Champion

"What makes this book distinctive and vital are the actionable insights for women in any country to grow their talents, opportunities, and visibility as leaders in their chosen sector(s) in our increasingly globally connected world."

Kare Anderson,
Author of Mutuality Matters

"This book helps women unlock their potential and excel as great leaders. The examples of inspiring women leaders reflect the author's passion for women leadership and his priority to achieve gender equality globally. Something desperately needed. It is a thought-provoking and inspiring book for women and men alike."

Michelle Tillis Lederman
Author The 11 Laws of Likability and The Connector's Advantage

"Professor M.S. Rao's book 'Strategies to Build Women Leaders Globally: Think Managers, Think Men; Think Leaders, Think Women' advocates gender equality globally. It offers a blueprint to build women CEOs globally. It outlines essential qualities for women CEOs. It calls upon men to empathize with women and extend their hands with a big heart to groom women as CEOs. I highly recommend you reading this book."

Terri Levine, PhD
Bestselling author of dozens of titles including, Turbo Charge
How To Transform Your Business As A Heart-repreneur®
www.heartrepreneur.com

QUOTES

"Gender equality is more than a goal in itself. It is a precondition for meeting the challenge of reducing poverty, promoting sustainable development and building good governance." —Kofi Annan

"I've learned that making a 'living' is not the same thing as 'making a life'."—Maya Angelou

"The size of your dreams must always exceed your current capacity to achieve them. If your dreams do not scare you, they are not big enough." —Ellen Johnson Sirleaf, *President of Liberia*

"Let hope unite us. Let humanity unite us. For hope and humanity is what the world can collectively give children – peace and prosperity is what future generations deserve. We must support efforts to focus on humanity, and overcome political and cultural divisions – prioritizing humanity, not war." —Nadia Murad

"Don't let others define you. Define yourself." —Virginia M. Rometty

"When I look into the future, it's so bright it burns my eyes." —Oprah Winfrey

"What really gives us hope is, above all, the capacity of the women we treat to recover." —Dr Denis Mukwege

"Sexual violence is a global problem that affects all humanity, not just women." —Dr Denis Mukwege

"Human rights are a universal standard. They are a component of every religion and every civilization." —Shirin Ebadi

"Emotion without action is irrelevant." —Jody Williams

"To say that on a daily basis you can make a difference, well you can! One act of kindness a day can do it." —Betty Williams

"Thirty years in the field has convinced me of one thing, the obvious fact that there are no answers from the top down. Governments do not have the answers. Indeed quite the reversal. A lot of times they not only do not have the answers, they themselves are the problem. If we are committed to helping our world's children, then we must begin to create solutions from the bottom up." —Betty Williams

"Nurture your mind with great thoughts; to believe in the heroic makes heroes." —Benjamin Disraeli

"I raise up my voice—not so I can shout, but so that those without a voice can be heard…we cannot succeed when half of us are held back." —Malala Yousafzai

"Every girl and every woman, has the potential to make this world a better place, and that potential lies in the act of thinking higher thoughts and feeling deeper things. When women and girls, everywhere, begin to see themselves as more than inanimate objects; but as beautiful beings capable of deep feelings and high thoughts, this has the capacity to create change all around. The kind of change that is for the better." —C. JoyBell C.

"A strong woman builds her own world. She is one who is wise enough to know that it will attract the man she will gladly share it with." —Ellen J. Barrier

"You can tell people the need to struggle, but when the powerless start to see that they really can make a difference, nothing can quench the fire." —Leymah Gbowee

"What lies behind you and what lies in front of you, pales in comparison to what lies inside of you." —Ralph Waldo Emerson

"Success is more permanent when you achieve it without destroying your principles." —Walter Cronkite

"Each person must live their life as a model for others." — Rosa Parks

"Life isn't just about taking in oxygen and giving out carbon dioxide." —Malala Yousafzai

"Memories of our lives, of our works and our deeds will continue in others." —Rosa Parks

"It is important to remember that we all have magic inside us." —J.K. Rowling

"My husband always tells me that I'm the most unrelenting person he's ever met, and it's true. If I make a commitment to something, I will stick to it no matter what." —Jenny Craig

"Running my own business is empowering. I get to set my own hours, call the shots, and contribute to my family." —Amanda Cookson

"Not that I would have listened, but I wish I'd known that it was okay to make mistakes earlier in my career. I went on to make some real doozies but I wish that rather than being embarrassed, which I was, I appreciated it was all part of learning and developing on the job." —Irene Chang Britt

"If one man can destroy everything, why can't one girl change it?" —Malala Yousafzai

"As women, we must stand up for ourselves. We must stand up for each other. We must stand up for justice for all." —Michelle Obama

"Never limit yourself because of others' limited imagination; never limit others because of your own limited imagination." —Mae Jemison

"Stand for something or you will fall for anything. Today's mighty oak is yesterday's nut that held its ground." —Rosa Parks

"A young mind is a powerful thing—full of imagination and big ideas that haven't yet been reined in by societal expectations, financial limitations, or the day-to-day stressors that bog down adults. But those minds need guidance to make their dreams a reality, and education is the support system that can get them there. With education, it's those minds that will change the world." —Ashley Mateo, Deputy Digital Editor, Shape.com

"Feeling a little uncomfortable with your skills is a sign of learning, and continuous learning is what the tech industry thrives on! It's important to seek out environments where you are supported, but where you have the chance to be uncomfortable and learn new things." —Vanessa Hurst, *Co-Founder of Girl Develop It*

"One thing I always tell young girls: Never let anybody tell you can't do it. Growing up, they'd look at me like, Really? Even when I did my college visit, I had someone tell me most people change their minds after the first year. I never gave up. Even when I was having teachers tell me, just take a break from math, you can take this class next year. I said, 'No, I'm going to take it now.' I kept pushing for it." —Michelle Haupt, Operations Engineer at NASA

"I've learned that time is my most valuable resource. How I spend it, where I spend it, and who I spend it with is the key to making me feel whole as a leader, parent, creative partner, and friend." —Andrea Jacobs

"Leadership is not a person or a position. It is a complex moral relationship between people based on trust, obligation, commitment, emotion, and a shared vision of the good." —Joanne Ciulla

"Work is love made visible. And if you can't work with love, but only with distaste, it is better that you should leave your work and sit at the gate of the temple and take alms of the people who work with joy" —Khalil Gibran

"Do not be afraid to make decisions. Do not be afraid to make mistakes." —Carly Fiorina

"Take criticism seriously, but not personally. If there is truth or merit in the criticism, try to learn from it. Otherwise, let it roll right off you." —Hillary Clinton

"Passion is energy. Feel the power that comes from focusing on what excites you." —Oprah Winfrey

"I think it's a combination of personality traits that have helped me to succeed. Not only hard work – but patience, sacrifice and choosing my battles have all helped me to reach the point in my career to which I aspired, in a company I admired." —Katelyn Gleason, *CEO of Eligible*

"'Restore connection' is not just for devices, it is for people too. If we cannot disconnect, we cannot lead." —Arianna Huffington

"My best successes came on the heels of failures." —Barbara Corcoran

"We must believe that we are gifted for something, and that this thing, at whatever cost, must be attained." —Marie Curie

"We need to reshape our own perception of how we view ourselves. We have to step up as women and take the lead." —Beyoncé

"Life shrinks or expands in proportion to one's courage." —Anais Nin

"Destiny is a name often given in retrospect to choices that had dramatic consequences." —J. K. Rowling

"Stop wearing your wishbone where your backbone ought to be." —Elizabeth Gilbert

"I have learned over the years that when one's mind is made up, this diminishes fear; knowing what must be done does away with fear." —Rosa Parks

"You cannot win without a workplace where women and men have equal opportunities, equal input, and equal power." —Dominic Barton

"Women-owned companies only receive a small slice of total venture capital funding. But what is surprising is how much more effective women-owned businesses are at turning a dollar of funding into a dollar of revenue – they generate better returns, and are ultimately a better bet. We hope that this research forms part of the case for change." —Katie Abouzahr

"It is unreasonable to think we can earn rewards without being willing to pay their true price. It is always our choice whether or not we wish to pay the price for life's rewards." —Epictetus

"Throw your dreams into space like a kite, and you do not know what it will bring back, a new life, a new friend, a new love, a new country." —Anaïs Nin

"When I dare to be powerful, to use my strength in the service of my vision, then it becomes less and less important whether I am afraid." —Audre Lorde

"Achievement seems to be connected with action. Successful men and women keep moving. They make mistakes but they don't quit." —Conrad Hilton

"The most difficult thing is the decision to act, the rest is merely tenacity. The fears are paper tigers. You can do anything you decide to do. You can act to change and control

your life; and the procedure, the process is its own reward."
—Amelia Earhart

"Just don't give up trying to do what you really want to do. Where there is love and inspiration, I don't think you can go wrong." —Ella Fitzgerald

"I tore myself away from the safe comfort of certainties through my love for truth – and truth rewarded me." — Simone de Beauvoir

"Odd how the creative power at once brings the whole universe to order." —Virginia Woolf

"I feel like young girls are told that they have to be a princess and fragile. It's bullshit. I identify much more with being a warrior – a fighter. If I was going to be a princess, I'd be a warrior princess." —Emma Watson

"A strong woman looks a challenge dead in the eye and gives it a wink." —Gina Carey

"Strategic leaders must not get consumed by the operational and tactical side of their work. They have a duty to find time to shape the future." —Stephanie S. Mead, CMOE

"I love those connections that make this big old world feel like a little village." —Gina Bellman

"Invisible threads are the strongest ties." —Friedrich Nietzsche

"Personal relationships are always the key to good business. You can buy networking; you can't buy friendships." —Lindsay Fox

"A great man shows his greatness by the way he treats little men." —Thomas Carlyle

"My philosophy is that not only are you responsible for your life, but doing the best at this moment puts you in the best place for the next moment." —Oprah Winfrey

"Surround yourself with a trusted and loyal team. It makes all the difference." — Alison Pincus

"If you don't like the way the world is, you change it. You have an obligation to change it. You just do it one step at a time." —Marian Wright Edelman

"I'm an ordinary person who found herself on an extraordinary journey. In sharing my story, I hope to help create space for other stories and other voices, to widen the pathway for who belongs and why." —Michelle Obama

"Taking joy in living is a woman's best cosmetic." —Rosalind Russell

"It is time for parents to teach young people early on that in diversity there is beauty and there is strength." —Maya Angelou

"I declare to you that woman must not depend upon the protection of man, but must be taught to protect herself, and there I take my stand." —Susan B. Anthony

"A woman in harmony with her spirit is like a river flowing. She goes where she will without pretense and arrives at her destination prepared to be herself and only herself." —Maya Angelou

"When you have more women on the board, is it making a difference? And the answer seems to be yes. Whatever metric you use, it seems that when there are more women—maybe it's greater diversity of thought that gets put into decision-making— you get better decision-making." —Jane Shaw, *Chairman of the Board of Directors of Intel*

"If you do things well, do them better. Be daring, be first, be different, be just." —Anita Roddick

"God gave women intuition and femininity. Used properly, the combination easily jumbles the brain of any man I've ever met." —Farrah Fawcett

"Never…stop at the boundaries of what you think your knowledge or training would suggest. If a problem grabs you, run with it and try to understand it from beginning to end, even if that means learning new techniques or developing them yourself." —Judith Rodin

"Always aim high, work hard, and care deeply about what you believe in. And, when you stumble, keep faith. And, when you're knocked down, get right back up and never listen to anyone who says you can't or shouldn't go on." —Hillary Clinton

"The right time to do the right thing is now." —Martin Luther King Jr

"Identity is cause; brand is effect, and the strength of the former influences the strength of the latter" —Larry Ackerman

"A great brand is a story that is never completely told." —Scott Bedbury

"In organizations, real power and energy is generated through relationships. The patterns of relationships and the capacities to form them are more important than tasks, functions, rules and positions." —Margaret Wheatley

"Our research indicates that when women work for female CEOs, they are more motivated to strive to be corporate leaders themselves. These results lead to the undeniable conclusion that if we really want gender equality at the top, we must promote more women into CEO positions and do it now." —Gail Heimann, *President, Weber Shandwick*

"It never, ever crossed my mind for one minute that what I'm doing now is what my life's work would be." —Andrea Kremer

"To be successful, you have to be able to relate to people; they have to be satisfied with your personality to be able to do business with you and to build a relationship with mutual trust." —George Ross

"Nothing liberates your greatness like the desire to help, the desire to serve." —Marianne Williamson

"Networking is by far the most important aspect of business school. The classroom is a distant second." —Jay Devivo

"If you want to go fast, go alone. If you want to go far, go with others." —African Proverb

"Without leaps of imagination, or dreaming, we lose the excitement of possibilities. Dreaming, after all, is a form of planning." —Gloria Steinem

"Negotiation in the classic diplomatic sense assumes parties more anxious to agree than to disagree." —Dean Acheson

"Whether you come from a council estate or a country estate, your success will be determined by your own confidence and fortitude." —Michelle Obama

"The single and most dangerous word to be spoken in business is no. The second most dangerous word is yes. It is possible to avoid saying either." —Lois Wyse

"It's a well-known proposition that you know who's going to win a negotiation; it's he who pauses the longest." —Robert Court

"Women are less likely than men to be mentored, and women of color get the least support of all." —Sheryl Sandberg

"Diplomacy is the art of letting someone else have your way." —Sir David Frost

"You have to persuade yourself that you absolutely don't care what happens. If you don't care, you've won. I absolutely promise you, in every serious negotiation, the man or woman who doesn't care is going to win." —Felix Dennis

"Don't think money does everything or you are going to end up doing everything for money." —Voltaire

"There is no great force for change, for peace, for justice and democracy, for inclusive economic growth than a world of empowered women." —Phumzile Mlambo-Ngcuka

"Achieving gender equality is about disrupting the status quo – not negotiating it." —Phumzile Mlambo-Ngcuka

"There are still many causes worth sacrificing for, so much history yet to be made." —Michelle Obama

"If men think that the way to address workplace sexual harassment is to avoid one-on-one time with female colleagues – including meetings, coffee breaks and all the interactions that help us work together effectively – it will be a huge setback for women." —Sheryl Sandberg

"If leaders want to unleash individual and collective talent, they must foster a psychologically safe climate where employees feel free to contribute ideas, share information, and report mistakes." —Amy Edmondson

"One individual can begin a movement that turns the tide of history." —Jack Canfield

"We cannot change what we are not aware of, and once we are aware, we cannot help but change." —Sheryl Sandberg

"To all the little girls who are watching, never doubt that you are valuable and powerful and deserving of every chance and opportunity in the world to pursue and achieve your own dreams." —Hillary Clinton

"There is no limit to what we, as women, can accomplish." —Michelle Obama

"I slept and I dreamed that life is all joy. I woke and I saw that life is all service. I served and saw that service is a joy." —Khalil Gibran

"Ones' philosophy is not best expressed in words; it's expressed in the choices one makes. In the long run, we shape our lives and we shape ourselves. The process never ends until we die. And, the choices we make are ultimately our own responsibility." —Eleanor Roosevelt

This book is dedicated to three inspiring women leaders—Rosa Parks, Maya Angelou, and Oprah Winfrey.

FOREWORD

भारत के उपराष्ट्रपति

VICE-PRESIDENT OF INDIA

MESSAGE

I extend my greetings and congratulation to Professor M.S. Rao, for his book "Strategies to Build Women Leaders Globally: Think Managers, Think Men; Think Leaders, Think Women"

Dedicated to great personalities namely Rosa Parks, Maya Angelou and Oprah Winfrey and issues associated with the empowerment of women, I hope that this book will provide a number of insights that will inspire many readers.

I congratulate Professor M.S. Rao.

(M. Venkaiah Naidu)

New Delhi
11th December, 2018

PREFACE

"You may encounter many defeats, but you must not be defeated. In fact, it may be necessary to encounter the defeats, so you can know who you are, what you can rise from, how you can still come out of it." —Maya Angelou

Welcome to *Strategies to Build Women Leaders Globally: Think Managers, Think Men; Think Leaders, Think Women.* This book on women leadership highlights the challenges women encounter to excel in their careers and reach C-level positions.

This book begins with the stories of three inspiring women leaders—Rosa Parks, Oprah Winfrey, and Malala Yousafzai who changed the world. It outlines research findings on gender differences and substantiates that women are better leaders than men. It debunks myths about women leaders. It differentiates between men and women leadership styles and communication styles. It unveils the tools and techniques to improve soft skills, networking skills, and negotiation skills. It shares the striking story of Indra Nooyi—'Leave the Crown in the Garage' and implores to encourage diversity and inclusion. It explains the causes that hold women leaders back. It implores to overcome 'Queen Bee' Syndrome to ensure C-level women executives. It reminds that women cannot have it all. It unveils sexual harassment in the workplace and advocates #MeToo movement to ensure safe workplaces. It explains the mind of the women CEOs and unfolds that the companies helmed by women leaders overcame organizational crises successfully. It offers strategies for women leaders to excel as chief executives. It explains the power of the network and advises to build a team of connections globally. It offers tips to leverage social media to fast-track your career. It emphasizes humanizing your leadership brand. It implores to break the glass ceiling to excel as CEOs.

Toward the end, it introduces soft leadership and explains women leadership. It explains 11 C's of "soft leadership"—character, charisma, conscience, conviction, courage, communication, compassion, commitment, consistency, consideration and contribution. It illustrates with inspiring examples of international leaders including Mahatma Gandhi, Mikhail Gorbachev, Martin Luther King Jr, Aung San Sui Kyi, Winston Churchill, Mother Teresa, Nelson Mandela, John Wesley, Dalai Lama, and Booker T. Washington. It compares soft leadership, servant leadership, and transformational leadership. It differentiates between the soft leadership and the hard leadership with examples. It concludes to acquire six characteristics—character, conscience, courage, compassion, commitment and contribution to excel as a successful woman leader and CEO.

I hope this book will inspire you to excel as a leader and CEO.

Professor M.S. Rao, Ph.D., #HeForShe

ACKNOWLEDGMENTS

Writing a book is never a solo project. I am deeply indebted to many people whose expertise, wisdom and encouragement kept me going. My wife's encouragement made this book possible. My wife, Padmavathy, is a symbol of sacrifice and support for my books and is also an immeasurable blessing in my life.

I thank everyone including the team of Waterside Productions, Inc for publication of this book. I specifically thank Bill Gladstone for his initiative, commitment, positive attitude and professionalism in the publication of this book. I thank all those behind the scenes – editors, production staff, and copyeditors – who have helped bring this work to life.

I would like to thank my coaching clients, who are among the most fantastic leaders. I have learned far more from them than they have learned from me.

I express special thanks to all my readers who graciously took time off from their busy schedules to write to me, share their views, and offer feedback on my books.

1 – ONE WOMAN CAN CHANGE THE WORLD

"Every great dream begins with a dreamer. Always remember, you have within you the strength, the patience, and the passion to reach for the stars to change the world."
—Harriet Tubman

When we think about managers we think about men. When we think about leaders do we think about women? We must think about women because women are better leaders than men in several aspects. Most men talk about women empowerment and equality of women but in reality, a few of them walk their talk and advocate gender equality globally. I have shown my commitment to advocating gender equality globally by signing up for the UN Women's #HeForShe initiative. I have written several articles on women empowerment in my books and blogs for more than a decade. I decided to author a book on women empowerment and leadership. Now the book is in your hands. Welcome to the book, *Strategies to Build Women Leaders Globally: Think Managers, Think Men; Think Leaders, Think Women.*

One Woman can Change the World

"You must never be fearful about what you are doing when it is right." —Rosa Parks

When you look at Rosa Parks, she was one woman who refused to give her bus seat to a white passenger thus setting the civil rights movement in America. When you look at Tarana Burke, she is one woman who is responsible for #MeToo Movement thus bringing waves globally. When you look at Oprah Winfrey, she is one woman who continues to inspire the world with her entrepreneurship and leadership. When you look at Malala Yousafzai she is one woman who refused to bow down to terrorists' bullets thus pioneering girls' education globally at the tender age of 10 years. And the list goes on with women leaders who changed the world and inspired us. It is obvious that one woman can make a difference. In this introductory chapter, we will discuss three women leaders who broke the glass ceiling and inspired millions of women and men globally.

Rosa Parks—Mother of the Civil Rights Movement

"Stand for something or you will fall for anything. Today's mighty oak is yesterday's nut that held its ground." —Rosa Parks

Rosa Parks, the "Mother of the Civil Rights Movement" refused to give up her bus seat to a white passenger that led to civil disobedience and nonviolent resistance to social injustice. On December 01 evening in 1955, Rosa Parks quietly incited a revolution—by just sitting down.

"Are you going to stand up?" Montgomery bus driver James Blake demanded. Rosa Parks looked straight at him and said: "No." Flustered, and not quite sure what to do, Blake retorted, "Well, I'm going to have you arrested." And Parks, still sitting next to the window, replied softly, "You may do that." After Parks refused to move, she was arrested and fined $10. She remarked, "I have no police record, I'd worked all my life, I wasn't pregnant with an illegitimate child. The white people couldn't point to me and say that there was anything I had done to deserve such treatment except to be born black". She spurred the Montgomery boycott and the chain of events changed the United States. Finally, the Supreme Court ruled segregation on buses was illegal in 1956. Rosa Parks was an inspiring woman who changed the face of the world by advocating civil rights. Here are some lessons you can learn from her. Be bold. Fight for your rights. Take your battle to its logical end.

Oprah Winfrey—An Inspiring Entrepreneur and Media Moghul

"The biggest adventure you can take is to live the life of your dreams." —Oprah Winfrey

Oprah Gail Winfrey needs no introduction to the world. She is a self-made billionaire with a huge presence on social media trending with hashtag #Oprah2020. She is a multifaceted personality—an entrepreneur, actress, television producer, talk show host, philanthropist, and an inspirational woman leader. She rose from humble origins and defied all odds to become rich and voice for women causes globally. She is emotional and eloquent. She was inspired by Maya Angelou's autobiography, "I Know Why the Caged Bird Sings." She considers Maya Angelou her mentor. She is a voracious reader and enjoys reading self-help books. She interviewed several eminent international celebrities including Michael Jackson in 'The Oprah Winfrey Show.' She received America's highest civilian honor, the Presidential Medal of Freedom from Barack Obama in November 2013. Here are some lessons you can learn from her. Dream big. Follow your passionate areas. Be a continuous learner. Lead from the front. Walk your talk. Leverage your strengths but be cautious about your weaknesses. Take risks and learn lessons from failures. Hire people smarter than you and give them credit. Work hard, smart and wise. Stay relevant. Build your credibility and enhance your visibility. Build your leadership brand consistently. Reinvent yourself. Stay grounded. Be magnanimous. Keep people before profit. Add value to others. Don't compromise with your principles. Be passionate about making a difference in the world.

Malala Yousafzai—An Inspiring Millennial

"We should not wait for someone else to come and raise our voice. We should do it by ourselves. We should believe in ourselves. Yes, we can do it. One day you will see that all the girls will be powerful; All the girls will be going to school. And it is possible only by our struggle; only when we raise our voice." —Malala Yousafzai

Malala Yousafzai is a bold Pakistani child activist who advocated girl child's right to education. She defied death threats from the Taliban and boldly spoke about the importance of education for girls in Pakistan. The Taliban attempted to silence her by shooting her on the morning of October 9, 2012. She survived and pioneered education for every child. She remarked, "They thought a bullet would silence us, but they failed. Nothing changed in my life except this: Weaknesses, fear and hopelessness died. Strength, power and courage was born." She was honored at the age of 15 on the cover of TIME's 100 Most Influential People. She is the youngest Nobel Peace Prize recipient. As a mark of respect to her, Malala Day is celebrated on 12th of July every year to highlight the fight of education globally. It is obvious from her biography that there is no cause too small to fight for. Here are some lessons you must learn from her. Dream big. Be bold. Step out of your comfort zone. Set an example. Lead from the front. Inspire others. Fight for your rights. Be persistent. Overcome obstacles. Be resilient. Age is not a deterrent to make a difference to the world. Remember, everything is possible in the world when you are determined and passionate about bringing the change. Malala is a true inspiration to the world better than the so-called celebrities who adopt all types of gimmicks to draw attention to market and brand themselves.

> The head of the UN agency[1] promoting equality for women is lamenting that a girl born today will be an 81-year-old grandmother before she has the same chance as a man to be CEO of a company – and she will have to wait until she is 50 to have an equal chance to lead a country.

---

1   https://www.theguardian.com/world/2015/mar/06/gender-equality-still-decades-away-un-women

Conclusion

"I believe we are here on the planet Earth to live, grow up and do what we can to make this world a better place for all people to enjoy freedom." —Rosa Parks

Drawing inspiration from these inspiring women leaders, women must break their mental barriers and limitations to become agents of change globally. To conclude, one woman can change the world. And that one woman is YOU!

"There is no chance, no destiny, no fate, that can hinder or control the firm resolve of a determined soul." —Ella Wheeler Wilcox

References

Author's Vision 2030: https://professormsraovision2030.blogspot.com

Author's Amazon URL: http://www.amazon.com/M.-S.-Rao/e/B00MB63BKM

Author's LinkedIn: https://in.linkedin.com/in/professormsrao

Author's You Tube: http://www.youtube.com/user/profmsr7

Author's Google Plus: https://plus.google.com/+ProfessorMSRao

Author's Facebook page: https://www.facebook.com/Professor-MS-Rao-451516514937414/

Author's Company Facebook Page: https://www.facebook.com/MSR-Leadership-Consultants-India-375224215917499/

Author's Instagram: https://www.instagram.com/professormsrao

Author's Blogs:

http://professormsraoguru.blogspot.com

http://professormsrao.blogspot.com

http://profmsr.blogspot.com

http://www.ushistory.org/us/54b.asp

https://www.nobelprize.org/prizes/peace/2014/yousafzai/autobiography/

https://www.theguardian.com/world/2015/mar/06/gender-equality-still-decades-away-un-women

2 – Think Managers, Think Men; Think Leaders, Think Women

"The glass ceiling that once limited a woman's career path has paved a new road towards business ownership, where women can utilize their sharp business acumen while building strong family ties." —Erica Nicole

Globally there are a few women who occupied the position of CEOs while most women culminated their careers in the middle-level management. In fact, very few women reach senior level management. Does it indicate that women lack the ambition to excel as CEOs? Is there any glass ceiling that prevents women from reaching the top positions? Are there any hidden reasons? Let us explore it from multiple perspectives to address this global challenge.

Research Findings

"Women attribute their success to working hard, luck, and help from other people. Men will attribute that – whatever success they have, that same success – to their own core skills." —Sheryl Sandberg

According to the Forbes Insights study with Grant Thornton[1], more women are occupying leadership positions in the Asia Pacific region and China. The research further shows that women occupying leadership is very promising globally. However, much needs to

---

1   www.grantthornton.cn/upload/IBR_2013_Women_in_senior_management_EN.pdf

be done to prepare women leaders for the C—level positions. The latest research findings[2] on women CEOs globally shows that only 6% of Fortune 500 CEOs are women, and most women CEOs were concentrated in utilities, consumer goods (including retail), and financial services (particularly insurance). How do we fix the problem? How do we improve the number?

There are certain gender issues that prevent women from reaching top positions such as maternity, raising children, taking care of the spouse and balancing with family to name a few. Although most men talk of women empowerment it remains in the letter only, not in the spirit. It is still unclear whether men feel insecure if women reach the top positions.

Although leadership is not gendered, we find only a few women leaders globally due to cultural, religious, social and other factors including glass ceiling. The good news is that currently women are kicking the glass ceiling and excelling globally to carve a niche for themselves. For instance, women leaders including Melinda Gates, Michelle Obama, Hillary Clinton, Angela Merkel, Indra Nooyi, Ursula Burns, Meg Whitman, and Sheryl Sandberg stood out from others due to their extraordinary contribution in their areas and became a source of inspiration for other women leaders. Despite several constraints, women are proving their credentials and capabilities on par with men. They are not behind in any way when compared with male leaders.

Research Findings on Gender Differences

"We started a women's forum. We got up to 500 people. The best of the women would come to me and say, "I don't want to be in this forum. I'm not in the victims' unit. I am a star. I want to be compared with the best of your best."." —John F. Welch

Research shows that women take failures to their heart and take a little longer time to move on from their failures. They are hard

---

2   https://engage.kornferry.com/womenceosspeak

on themselves and love to be perfectionists. They fail to claim their achievements and make noise publicly especially on social media because of gender and cultural aspects. Additionally, they fail to leverage their networks and groups thus hindering their career prospects. Women fail to network for fear of being misunderstood by others. Women often ruminate about their failures more than men. They are harder on themselves than men. They are better in multitasking than men.

Research shows that women speak an average of 20,000 words a day while men typically speak around 7,000. Terence Jackson, Ph.D., a C-Suite Advisor comments, "While conducting research for a presentation I was giving to the top 20 Women leaders at NY Life, I discovered some interesting information. While analyzing a data set of over 60,000 leaders, I determined that women outperform men in 13 of the 16 most differentiating leadership competencies. In fact, they outperformed their male counterparts in overall effectiveness with every rater group, i.e. peers, direct reports, manager. The largest effectiveness ratings gap occurred in feedback from the leaders' managers. On average, women outperformed men by almost five percent! The data is clear that ability is not the issue. Women can, and often do, perform well in leadership positions."

Research further shows that compared to men, women are better at interpersonal skills, soft skills, emotional intelligence, empathy, flexibility, and sociability. In a 2017 survey, Deloitte found that organizations with diverse and inclusive cultures tend to be six times more innovative, six times more agile in anticipating and responding to change, and twice as likely to meet or exceed financial targets. Organizations truly committed to gender diversity look at if not as a means of virtue signaling, but something as important as any business issue. It is observed that women get senior positions when companies are in a downturn and riddled with challenges. It is obvious that women can troubleshoot effectively and can lead during crises effectively. Series of experimental studies (Ryan and Haslam, 2005) showed that a female candidate is more likely to be appointed to a leadership position when the position is risky and there is an increased risk of failure. The technology provider, SAP is committed to promoting women to leadership roles and responsibilities. It has experienced significant growth in profitability and margin by empowering women.

Strengths of Women

"A woman is like a tea bag, you can't tell how strong she is until you put her in hot water." —Eleanor Roosevelt

Women work harder than men to prove themselves in the male-dominated corporate world. They don't like to be scapegoated by male leaders. Hence, they definitely work harder than men. They stand up for they believe in and work with flexibility and adaptability. They are collaborative while men are competitive by nature. Collaboration is essential for the smooth functioning of organizations and equally essential is a competitive spirit without which organizations cannot succeed. Blending both collaboration and competition is essential to achieve organizational excellence and effectiveness. Here are some strengths about women: Biologically women have a huge potential and are compassionate by nature. They empathize with others and are sensitive to others' feelings. They are expert in interpersonal skills and soft skills. They can handle stress better than men. By nature, men are aggressive. However, women are soft and well-behaved. Women are also expert in hidden data of communication. That is why they know the knack of understanding male egos, emotions, and feelings better and act accordingly. Women are leaders at home. They lead their spouses and children effectively. They are more responsible toward work.

Women have tenacity, patience, and perseverance. They can multi-task. They can bounce back from failures with tenacity and resilience. However, they must unlock their potential by breaking the boundaries. They must raise their bar. They must avoid looking for approval and validation. They must be prepared to fail and learn lessons from them. Above all, they must be proud of being women.

Boards with more women are more ethical, companies with more women on executive committees bring in more revenue, and balancing a team of men with women lifts the collective intelligence of the group.

Are Women Better Leaders than Men?

"You gain strength, courage and confidence by every experience in which you really stop to look fear in the face. You are able to say to yourself, "I lived through this horror. I can take the next thing that comes along." You must do the thing you think you cannot do." —Eleanor Roosevelt

There is a debate globally about whether women are better leaders than men. A research study[3] by Jack Zenger and Joseph Folkman shows that the majority of leaders (64%) are still men. Their study substantiates that women are better than men in various aspects. Women have several strengths to their credit and the major six aspects include taking initiative; practicing self-development; displaying high integrity and honesty; driving for results; developing others; and inspiring and motivating others. However, women have more challenges than men as they must manage their family, take care of children and do other household chores. Additionally, they encounter organizational politics, gender discrimination and sexual harassment in the workplace.

Women are basically leaders because it is a well-admitted fact that behind the success of every man there is a woman. Historically, most women led behind the scenes by guiding men. D.M. Timney rightly remarked, "The king may rule the kingdom, but it's the queen who moves the board." Businesses can also improve if they encourage women to lead because they can bring in lots of value to the table.

3   https://hbr.org/2016/04/do-women-make-bolder-leaders-than-men

There is a strong perception that men are promoted due to potential while women are promoted due to performance. It is basically because leadership is synonymous with men, not women. Hence, there must be a shift in the attitude and perception of the people toward leadership and women. Both men and women leaders are two sides of the same coin and the coin is incomplete without anyone. Hence, leadership is incomplete without the active participation of women leaders. Global Inc must spot, support and groom women to keep them in the leadership pipeline to improve organizational bottom lines.

"A woman with a voice is by definition a strong woman. But the search to find that voice can be remarkably difficult." —Melinda Gates

References

www.grantthornton.cn/upload/IBR_2013_Women_in_senior_management_EN.pdf

https://engage.kornferry.com/womenceosspeak

https://hbr.org/2016/04/do-women-make-bolder-leaders-than-men

https://www.ddiworld.com/DDI/media/trend-research/holding-women-back_tr_ddi.pdf?ext=.pdf

https://images.dowjones.com/wp-content/uploads/sites/137/2017/07/31153316/WITW_2015_JournalReport.pdf

https://www.deakinco.com/uploads/news/Anneli_Blundell_white-paper.pdf

3 – Myths and Truths About Women Leaders

"Each time a woman stands up for herself, she stands up for all women." —Maya Angelou

Myths are major challenges globally. They are unrealities that hold the people back. They create wrong assumptions leading to wrong conclusions. They adversely affect society. Hence, they must be debunked with facts and figures. When you look at women and women leaders, there are several myths that prevent them from contributing their best. They prevent them from achieving success. In this chapter, we will discuss debunking myths about women and women leaders.

Myths and Truths About Women Leaders
"The great enemy of the truth is very often not the lie, deliberate, contrived and dishonest, but the myth, persistent, persuasive and unrealistic." —John F. Kennedy

There are several myths associated with women and women leaders. Here are some myths with truths about them.

Myth #1: Women are not ambitious.
Truth: Women are equally ambitious like men but they are more relationship-oriented, unlike men who are more task-oriented. Women care for their family and children. Hence, it is improper to label them as non-ambitious.

Myth #2: Advancement of women leaders is a threat for men leaders.

Truth: Usually men often compete with men while advancing their careers. With the entry of women leaders, men must compete with men and women while advancing their careers. There is no change in competition except the gender. There is nothing to be concerned as long as men are strong in their knowledge, skills, and abilities.

Myth #3: All men are against women empowerment.

Truth: No. Only a few men are against women empowerment who cannot digest the fact that women should be treated equally to men in all aspects. It takes time for them to empathize and understand to respect women and empower them finally. Additionally, there are some men who encourage women empowerment and advocate gender equality globally—#HeForShe.

Myth #4: Women cannot execute tasks effectively.

Truth: The truth is that women can execute tasks effectively and can also multitask, unlike men who can execute one task at a time effectively.

Myth #5: Women cannot lead.

Truth: Leadership is not gender related. Anyone can lead irrespective of his or her community, creed, caste, color and gender. Kathleen Schafer rightly remarked, "Leadership is not about men in suits. It is a way of life for those who know who they are and are willing to be their best to create the life they want to live."

Myth #6: Women are unsuitable to occupy senior positions.

Truth: Women are equal to men and can occupy all positions and handle issues with a cool demeanor. When you look at Indra Nooyi she proved as a successful CEO for PepsiCo for many years.

Myth #7: Women are unfit for some military roles and operations.

Truth: Although women have certain biological health issues, they can contribute the way men contribute. Hence, gender is not an excuse to deny them equal opportunities to serve in the military.

Myth #8: Women burst under pressure.

Truth: In fact, women can work under pressure better than men. Men often burst when they are under pressure whereas women remain calm and composed under pressure. Additionally, women explore ideas rather than to brood over issues, unlike men.

Myth #9: Women cannot manage money.

Truth: It is only a perception that women spend money carelessly on shopping. But they are more cautious while spending money. They look for value for their money and are better investors than men. Men are often emotional while investing money while women are often analytical while investing money.

Myth #10: Women are part of the problem.

Truth: In fact, women are part of the solution. When men create problems women create solutions to overcome them.

Myth #11: Women must remain at home.

Truth: That was the philosophy in Stone Age, not now. Women must come out of their homes to lead and provide better directions to the societies. No society can grow without the support of women. In fact, behind the success of every man, there is a woman. It is obvious that women lead at the home. Margaret Thatcher once remarked, "Any woman who understands the problems of running a home will be nearer to understanding the problems of running a country." Imagine the kind of world we would create when women come out and lead outside with men.

> Series of experimental studies[1] showed that a female candidate is more likely to be appointed to a leadership position when the position is risky and there is an increased risk of failure.

Conclusion

"There is no force equal to a woman determined to rise." —W.E.B. Dubois

There must be a change in the mindset of the men about women and women leaders. Men must change their attitude and perceptions toward women. They must understand the ground realities and understand the advantages of encouraging women to lead in all the fronts to build a better world. To conclude, debunk the myths to empower women and ensure the participation of women to create gender equality globally and build a prosperous world.

"No country can ever truly flourish if it stifles the potential of its women and deprives itself of the contributions of half of its citizens." —Michelle Obama

Reference

https://www.ncbi.nlm.nih.gov/pmc/articles/PMC4641904/

---

1   https://www.ncbi.nlm.nih.gov/pmc/articles/PMC4641904/

4 – Women versus Men Leadership Styles

"There is nothing like a concrete life plan to weigh you down. Because if you always have one eye on some future goal, you stop paying attention to the job at hand, miss opportunities that might arise, and stay fixedly on one path, even when a better, newer course might have opened up." —Indra Nooyi

Leadership is fundamentally based on individual, environment, and situation. Although leadership is leadership, it differs between person to person and between men and women. The way people lead is different from leader to leader. The way women lead is different from men. Women leaders emphasize more on democratic process to build consensus. They make decisions after weighing all options by thinking coolly. They emphasize more on collaboration, not competition. They are empathetic and good listeners. They apply different strokes to different men as all men are not alike. However, they don't take many risks like men. Here is some characteristic of women that make them lead differently from men. Women are tender, moral, cooperative and trustworthy. They are imaginative, empathetic and open to listening from all sources. They give more importance to emotions and feelings. They emphasize inspirational motivation and adopt transformational leadership style in the workplace to accomplish organizational objectives. In a nutshell, they adopt more of transformational leadership than transactional leadership and more soft leadership than hard leadership.

> Women believe more in transformational rather than transactional leadership. They cooperate and collaborate with others. They demonstrate flexibility and adaptability respecting others with empathy.

Facts[1] about Women

Here are some facts about women. Women constitute half of the global population. They make decisions at home about buying and it is a great opportunity for businesses to target this gender. Their education is increasing and longevity is higher. They improve organizational bottom lines. A minimum of three women on the board gave the best results. Companies with more women on their boards see better corporate governance and ethical behavior. Investing in women leaders has great effects on a country's GDP and the welfare of next generations. The Third Billion – a billion women will enter the global economy by 2020.

Deborah Tannen[2], an established communications specialist, has specialized in gender-specific communication in the workplace, to which she refers to as rituals. Men and women tend to communicate in different ways. Increased awareness and an understanding from both sides are crucial for career success. Consider the following powerful example based on Gloria Feldt's (a renowned gender expert) interview with Deborah Tannen.

A married couple is driving a car when the wife asks "would you like some coffee", the husband responds with "No, Thank you." The wife would have liked coffee herself, so she perceives his answer as an order she has to accept and continues the journey resenting him for not considering her needs. Later, when the husband notices his wife's annoyance, he is irritated

---

1   http://www.cpahq.org/cpahq/cpadocs/Genderdiffe.pdf
2   http://www.cpahq.org/cpahq/cpadocs/Genderdiffe.pdf

that she did not just say what she needed. For him, the conversation is an exchange of information. For her, it is a path to negotiation.

Challenges[3] for Women

Women find it hard to network with senior-level executives who are mostly men. Here are some challenges women encounter to fast-track their careers:

- Men benefit from the association between stereotypical male values and leadership. Double standards in the way men and women's performance & potential is assessed.
- Men tend to be promoted based on potential whereas women are promoted based on experience.
- Men talk over or don't hear what women say. Well-motivated men make decisions for women that may 'kill careers with kindness.'
- Men's networks sideline women.

Men must change their perceptions toward women and support them to overcome the challenges women encounter to achieve gender-equal society. They must appreciate the fact that women add excellence and elegance to the boards. Hence, men must encourage women to participate on boards and to become CEOs.

Strategies for Women to Fast-track Their Careers

Laura D. Tyson, a professor of business administration and economics at the University of California (Berkeley) and co-author of the WEF report, states that "A nation's competitiveness depends significantly on whether and how it educates and utilizes its female talent. To maximize its competitiveness and development potential, each country should strive for gender equality — i.e., to give women the same rights, responsibilities,

---

3   https://www.murrayedwards.cam.ac.uk/sites/default/files/
    Collaborating%20with%20Men%20-%20FINAL%20Report.pdf

and opportunities as men. In the current global financial and economic crisis, it is more vital than ever that women's economic participation does not shrink, but is in fact seen as an opportunity to make headway."

Women must not hesitate to promote and brand themselves. They must express their ambitions to achieve career success. The list to fast-track women's career is lengthy. However, here is a list of some strategies for women to fast-track their careers:

- Identify your talents to unlock your potential. Build skills around your talents and leverage them effectively to build your leadership brand.
- Avoid playing gender card or victim card. Be part of the solution, not the problem. Identify your own ways to follow the road less traveled to leave your mark behind.
- Don't hesitate to network with others. Remember, more display means more sales. The more visibility you have, the more opportunities you have.
- Being persuasive helps you. But being an effective negotiator helps you more and takes you toward your goals quickly.
- Invest your money, energy and time to acquire education regularly. Having right mentors help you greatly to hit the bull's eye.
- Explore sponsors who can fund you or assist you financially to accomplish your goals.
- Join relevant and appropriate professional groups and network to increase your influence.

Above all, remember that the change must begin within. If you can bring the change within yourself, you will be able to bring the change in others.

"When women are at the table, good things happen: the discussion is richer, the decision-making process is better, management is more innovative and collaborative and the organization is stronger." —Joe Keefe President and CEO of Pax World Management

References

http://www.cpahq.org/cpahq/cpadocs/Genderdiffe.pdf

https://www.murrayedwards.cam.ac.uk/sites/default/files/
Collaborating%20with%20Men%20-%20FINAL%20Report.pdf

5 – Women versus Men Communication Styles

"Whenever you're in conflict with someone, there is one factor that can make the difference between damaging your relationship and deepening it. That factor is attitude."
—William James

Conflicts occur in all aspects of our life. They cannot be eliminated completely. However, they can be minimized to a great extent, if adequate precautionary measures are taken. Approaches to addressing the conflicts differ between the genders and on the situation. Hence, we will explore the gender differences, communication styles and the addressing conflicts amicably.

Whenever conflicts arise women act differently from men. In fact, women act while men react to conflicts. Men often settle their scores instantly while women take a little longer time to settle their scores. While men forget most of their negative experiences, women remember and ruminate about them. It is a well-admitted fact that men share negative experiences, observations, and information with a few of their close connections while women share with more connections. Hence, there is a possibility of women spreading information more than men. Research shows that women feel at home through connection while men feel at home through conflict. John Gray outlines in his book, *Men are From Mars and Women are From Venus* as follows: "Men mistakenly expect women to think, communicate, and react the way men do; women mistakenly expect men to feel, communicate, and respond the way women do. We have forgotten that men and women are supposed to be different. As a result, our relationships are filled with unnecessary friction and conflict."

Men versus Women

"The Law of Win/Win says, "Let's not do it your way or my way; let's do it the best way." —Greg Anderson

The communication styles differ from person to person and between genders. Here are some differences between women and men in their approaches toward resolving conflicts. Women seek more information than men to arrive at their conclusions. They can decode and encode data more effectively than men. They are more emotional than men and enjoy talking more than men. They often see things from multiple perspectives, unlike men who often see from own their perspective. Women are indirect while men are direct in their approaches. Women use cell phones more than men and text more than men.

Research shows that humans demonstrate more than 10,000 facial expressions. But women use more facial expressions than men. Women are less likely to interrupt others. Women smile more often than men. Women are often more demanding than men and it is challenging to please women. Women are more relationship-oriented than men while men are more task-oriented than women. Women seek more details to come to their conclusions while men get straight to the point with their conclusions. Women are more effective in gauging the non-verbal cues than men. Above all, women are more assertive while men are more aggressive in their communication styles. Understanding these differences help you address conflicts effectively. To avoid miscommunication, you must consider asking the following questions:

- "I'm not sure I understood what you just said. Could you say that again using different words?"

- "What you just said hurt my feelings. I don't think that was your intention. Was it?"
- "I'm feeling really defensive right now. Let's take a minute because I don't like when I get so defensive."

Whenever there was a miscommunication, change your approach, not your attitude; attack the issues, not individuals. While addressing conflicts both genders must note that neither aggressiveness nor submissiveness works but it is the assertiveness that works. Hence, be proactive to overcome the conflicts and be assertive to address the conflicts to resolve them amicably.

American Journal of Political Science[1] ranked women as more effective lawmakers. Their biological predispositions give them advantages: women leaders tend to adopt more accommodating strategies, while men are more exploitive.

Conclusion

"The most difficult thing in any negotiation, almost, is making sure that you strip it of the emotion and deal with the facts." —Howard Baker

The differences between genders make approaches to resolving conflicts differently. Hence, both men and women must understand gender differences and adopt their styles according to the situation to address conflicts and ensure smooth communication to achieve organizational productivity and performance.

"If we manage conflict constructively, we harness its energy for creativity and development." —Kenneth Kaye

---

1   https://pdfs.semanticscholar.org/4698/d2a6dfa8bd81975d8a20
    707c7157f95c6e97.pdf

References

https://www.coastal.edu/media/administration/.../pdf/Cinardo_
Communication.pdf

http://www.uky.edu/ofa/sites/www.uky.edu.ofa/files/uploads/
Gender%20Styles%20in%20Communication.pdf

https://pdfs.semanticscholar.org/4698/d2a6dfa8bd81975d8a2070
7c7157f95c6e97.pdf

6 – Encourage Inclusion and Diversity

"Leadership is hard to define and good leadership even harder. But if you can get people to follow you to the ends of the earth, you are a great leader." —Indra Nooyi

With the stepping down of Indra Nooyi as the CEO of PepsiCo, the spotlight is thrown on women leaders in the C-level positions. The number of women CEOs in Fortune 500 has come down from 32 in 2017 to 24 in 2018. Here is a list of six women chief executives who have been replaced by men recently. Indra Nooyi, CEO at PepsiCo has been replaced by Ramon Laguarta; Denise M. Morrison at Campbell Soup has been replaced by Keith McLoughlin; Margo Georgiadis at the toy company Mattel has been replaced by Ynon Kreiz; Sherilyn S. McCoy at Avon has been replaced by Jan Zijderveld; Irene Rosenfeld at Mondelez has been replaced by Dirk Van de Put; and Meg Whitman at Hewlett-Packard has been replaced by Antonio Neri. These developments are shocking to digest; shaking the confidence of women leaders; and causing concern for women leaders globally. They discourage women empowerment and demotivate the women aspiring to reach C-level positions. It is a cause for concern and must be addressed immediately to ensure women participation in organizations to achieve gender equality globally. One of the main reasons cited for their stepping was their poor performance. Most reasons are not revealed.

In this chapter, we will identify the reasons and explore solutions to ensure the participation of women in senior level positions.

There are several reasons for the low-level participation of women in C-suite positions. Some of them include high pressure and stress levels. Women are more relationship-oriented than men and care for more relations thus undermining their positions as leaders and adversely affecting their career advancement. Women have different biological issues and challenges. They take the break for motherhood and care for their children and spouse. They find it tough to manage board politics and pressures. They often lack the adequate soft skills to handle the people on the board. They don't get encouraging support from all stakeholders. At times, boards don't support women wholeheartedly leading to their exit.

Indra Nooyi's Story—Leave the Crown in the Garage

Indra Nooyi's shared the following story after having been named as the President of PepsiCo.

I'll never forget coming home after being named President of PepsiCo back in 2001. My mother was visiting at the time.

"I've got great news for you," I shouted. She replied, "It can wait. We need you to go out and get some milk."

So I go out and get milk. And when I come back, I'm hopping mad. I say, "I had great news for you. I've just been named President of PepsiCo. And all you want me to do is go out and get milk."

Then she says, "Let me explain something to you. You may be President of PepsiCo. But when you step into this house, you're a wife and mother first. Nobody can take that place. So leave that crown in the garage."

Women and Boards

"I think society has, for centuries, trained us to think in certain ways about women and girls. It will take a long time, and it will take a persistent effort, to overcome those innate biases." —Anne Richards, CEO, M&G Investments

The boards that are led by women leaders have fewer scandals and more transparency. They improve the organizational bottom lines. A Peterson Institute[1] study found that having women on corporate boards and in the C-suite may contribute to firm performance and that among profitable companies, a move from no women leaders to 30 percent representation was associated with a 15 percent jump in profit.

It is challenging to analyze and understand why boards don't encourage women at the helm when they know that the women lead effectively and improve the financial performance. It seems something is wrong somewhere. Probably the boards must change their perception toward women leaders and view them as assets. Most global businesses have had some kind of formal gender diversity initiative in place for several years but they are ineffective.

Encourage Inclusion and Diversity

"I'm optimistic for women because if you look at the world going forward, technology has enabled jobs to be much more portable. That means we now have much greater competition for talent. Talent will reach out beyond geography." —Jennifer Johnson

Here are some steps to achieve gender diversity at C-levels.

- Provide a healthy organizational culture. Promote an inclusive culture that encourages diversity.
- Provide flex time, work from home, parental leave, childcare subsidies, and on-premises childcare.
- Apply different strokes to both genders to achieve gender equality.
- Conduct employee surveys to identify the hidden bias and challenges that women encounter and address them earnestly.

It is a well-admitted fact that the diversified and balanced workforce leads to better financial returns. The diversity balance in the

---

1   https://www.vox.com/policy-and-politics/2018/6/8/17413254/
     women-fortune-500-ceos-politics-blue-wave

boardroom produces both financial and strategic rewards. Above all, women-led companies often perform better than C-suites dominated by men.

> Ultimately, it is the competence, not the gender that takes to the corner office. Hence, women must work hard, smart and wise to prove and establish themselves to accomplish their ambitions and fast-track career.

Conclusion

"We have to keep fighting the good fight to develop women, to mentor them, to support them, so that we can get more highly qualified women — and there's plenty of them — into the boardroom, into C suites and into the ultimate CEO job. My job is in fact just beginning once I leave PepsiCo because I can do things now that I was constrained to do when I was CEO of the company."
—Indra Nooyi

Women must understand that there is no free lunch in the world. They must slog hard to establish themselves instead of playing the gender card. They must acquire knowledge, skills, and abilities and reinvent regularly to stay relevant and competent to reach top positions.

There is no magic wand to achieve gender equality at C-levels in global organizations. In fact, the journey to the corner office is very challenging for both men and women leaders. But it is more challenging for women leaders with lots of limitations and constraints. It is a long and difficult process indeed! Hence, we must take small steps but firm steps to encourage women to scale the senior positions. Both men and women must collaborate to achieve it. Imagine if women who constitute almost half of the global population contribute with access to education and opportunities, we would build a world full of prosperity.

"Being a CEO requires strong legs and I feel like I ran two legs of a relay race and I want somebody else with nice strong legs and sharp eyes to come and lead this company." —Indra Nooyi

References

https://www.asianmoneyguide.com/life-lessons-pepsico

https://www.vox.com/policy-and-politics/2018/6/8/17413254/women-fortune-500-ceos-politics-blue-wave

www.rbc.com/newsroom/_assets .../pdf/Developing-Advancing-Female-Leaders.pdf

7 – Challenges Holding Women Leaders Back

"I didn't spend a lot of time thinking about as a woman how I would manage differently. There are lots of things I can change but my gender is not one of them, and so it is what it is. I have to lead according to my personality, according to what I think is necessary under any set of circumstances."
—Meg Whitman

There are several factors that are holding women leaders back within global organizations—stereotypes, structural obstacles, lifestyle issues, institutional mindsets, and individual mindsets to name a few. There are several barriers for the advancement of women leaders including glass ceiling, prejudices, the old boy network, gender discrimination, sexual harassment and lack of mentors to name a few. Research shows that women are less consulted and receive less recognition than men in organizations. Here are some reasons that are holding women back to reach senior level positions. C-suite women executives express that their gender cost promotion. Most women don't aspire to avoid the pressure and stress at the top level. Most women work in staff roles, not line roles thus losing out in the race to the top.

> According to a report by Lean In and McKinsey & Company[1] called Women in the Workplace, if the current, slow rate of progress over the last three years continues, it will take 25 years to reach "gender parity" at the senior VP level and more than 100 years to reach parity in the C-suite.

Overcoming the Conundrum

"Woman must not accept; she must challenge. She must not be awed by that which has been built up around her; she must reverence that woman in her which struggles for expression." —Margaret Sanger

It is a fact that women outperform men consistently in all aspects including curricular and extracurricular activities. Here are some solutions to overcome the challenges.

- Offer equal access to developmental experiences that would prepare women for senior levels.
- Make HR policies women-friendly. HR feedback helps them assess and improve themselves.
- Encourage mixed-gender management teams.

Women must smash through the glass ceiling. They must not shy away from shouldering responsibilities. They must stay in the game by learning and leading. They must break structural obstacles and build connections to fast-track their careers. Ritch K. Eich in his book, *Leadership CPR: Resuscitating the Workplace Through Civility, Performance and Respect* outlines three ways to ensure that women participate as fully in your organization as their male counterparts— don't assume women aren't interested in the same opportunities as men simply because they might one day leave the workforce to have a family. That is their decision to make, not yours; establish formal

---

1   https://limitless.insead.edu/7-deadly-myths/

programs in which men and women mentor one another equally; and make a commitment to champion women. Such a commitment will lead to a more balanced board and leadership team and will ultimately enhance your organization's competitive position in the marketplace. He offers five ideas organizations can implement to encourage women to serve on boards: make the commitment to diversify your board, stop stereotyping; many boards still run on the old model of leadership—command and control; most of the women the Ritch K. Eich has worked with have been better at multitasking than have men; and women are often told they don't have the right mix of experience to serve on a board.

Global companies including Bank of America, Citigroup, Goldman Sachs, J.P. Morgan, Morgan Stanley, and Wells Fargo are trying to close the gender gap at the top. Bruce Cleaver, CEO, De Beers Group said, "At De Beers, we recognize that we will only be able to realize our full potential by harnessing diversity of thought, skills, and experience. While we are in the early stages of our journey towards gender parity, I am proud to represent De Beers as a HeForShe Thematic Champion, and we are committed to accelerating the representation of women within our organization. Through our partnership with UN Women, we will invest in a range of programmes that help improve the prospects for women and girls in our partner communities, and we will run creative campaigns with empowering content, helping to ensure that women and girls benefit from diamonds at each stage of the value chain."

Conclusion

"I feel there is something unexplored about women that only a woman can explore." —Georgia O'Keeffe

Previously people talked about the biological differences between men and women. However, presently they are vocal about other issues including women empowerment, equality, and pay parity. It is obvious that there is a dramatic shift in the expectations and aspirations of women leaders. Hence, global organizations must address the causes that hold women back earnestly to empower women to achieve organizational excellence and effectiveness.

"At the end of the day, both men and women who become CEOs have shown tenacity and hard work to succeed in their careers. It takes not just skills but also extreme dedication and commitment. And regardless of gender, CEOs are measured by the same criteria – the growth and success of the business." —Susan Wojcicki

References

https://limitless.insead.edu/7-deadly-myths/ http://www.heforshe.org/en/newsroom/news/champions-announcement-2017

https://www.amazon.com/Leadership-CPR-Resuscitating-Workplace-Performance-ebook/dp/B07CY4CSRH

Leadership CPR: Resuscitating the Workplace Through Civility, Performance, and Respect by Ritch K. Eich (Redwood Publishing, LLC, May 7, 2018)

8 – Overcome 'Queen Bee' Syndrome

"Women don't help other women nearly enough at work."
—Indra Nooyi

Women encounter several challenges to establish and become successful. Mostly they encounter challenges from their male superiors and colleagues. In some cases, they encounter challenges especially suppression from the same sex which is known as 'Queen Bee' Syndrome. Cecilia Harvey, a London-based consultant and founder of global showcase platform Tech Women Today unfolds, "Queen Bees are adult versions of the mean girls from school—but now they have grown up and are more calculating. These socially aggressive behaviors include gossiping, social exclusion, social isolation, social alienation, talking about someone, and stealing friends or romantic partners." The derogatory[1] "queen bee" label is given to women who pursue individual success in male-dominated work settings (organizations in which men hold most executive positions) by adjusting to the masculine culture and by distancing themselves from other women. It is obvious that queen bees are the successful senior women who don't allow other ambitious princesses to succeed in the workplace. Worse, they prevent young women from reaching the senior positions. Their attitude and approach hurt

---

1   https://ppw.kuleuven.be/cscp/documents/artikels-colette/the-queen-bee-phenomenon.pdf

the interests of other ambitious young women leading to decreased morale and increased litigations within the organizations. Their behavior adversely affects organizational performance and productivity. Therefore, Queen Bee Syndrome can be defined as the practice where the successful senior women prevent ambitious princesses from reaching the senior positions.

Professor Allison Gabriel[2] remarked, "Women are ruder to each other than they are to men, or than men are to women. This isn't to say men were off the hook or they weren't engaging in these behaviors. But when we compared the average levels of incivility reported, female-instigated incivility was reported more often than male-instigated incivility by women in our three studies." The examples of queen bees include Margaret Thatcher and Indira Gandhi who were former Prime Ministers to UK and India respectively. In traditional Indian society, mothers-in-law usually turn out queen bees for their daughters-in-law.

> Women in positions of power can be punishing toward women below them in their organizations. These queen bees tend to see other women as foes to be thwarted.

Causes for Turning into Queen Bees

"The 'Queen Bee Syndrome' is pervasive—and it's not new." —Lisa A. Rossbacher

Research shows that women are meaner to each other than they are to their men. They are more ambitious to fast-track their careers than to advance the careers of their female colleagues and subordinates. There are several reasons for women turning into queen bees. They want young women to struggle and suffer because they struggled and suffered to reach their senior positions. They lack empathy and sympathy toward the same gender. They turn out to

---

2   https://www.bustle.com/p/what-is-queen-bee-syndrome-it-might-explain-why-some-women-are-uncivil-to-each-other-at-work-8402852

be hard and their leadership style becomes autocratic. There may be psychological reasons, their personality type, and the environment in which they were brought up. At times, they behave themselves more like men and distance themselves from other women thus endorsing glass ceiling. A few women turn into queen bees to flow along with the male stream to fast-track their careers.

Conclusion

"Women aren't any meaner to women than men are to one another. Women are just expected to be nicer." —Sheryl Sandberg

Queen Bee Syndrome is a controversial topic that cannot be substantiated with research findings because it is based on perceptions. It may be a generational perception rather than a gender perception. Hence, it is essential to bust the myth that there is something inherent in women that hinders the growth of other women. Queen bees are bred, not born.

Queen bees must learn that great leaders pave the way for others by laying the ladder. To empower women and ensure their career advancement, we need righteous women, not queen bees. The young women must not give up their goals when odds are stacked against them including from the same sex. They must demonstrate their grit and determination to excel in all aspects of life to leave their marks for others to follow. To conclude, there is a need for righteous women who can mentor and support other young women to grow as leaders to close the gender gap at the top.

"There is a special place in hell for women who don't help other women." —Madeleine Albright

References

https://ppw.kuleuven.be/cscp/documents/artikels-colette/the-queen-bee-phenomenon.pdf

https://www.bustle.com/p/what-is-queen-bee-syndrome-it-might-explain-why-some-women-are-uncivil-to-each-other-at-work-8402852

9 – Soft Skills Training for Women Leaders

"I have learned people will forget what you said. People will forget what you did, but people will never forget how you make them feel." —Maya Angelou

Soft skills are essential for everyone irrespective of rank, position, and gender. They are essential, especially for women to excel as leaders and C-level executives. There is a myth that soft skills are closely connected with gender. The truth is that soft skills are not gender related. They are essential from janitors to the highest positions in the organizations. In this chapter, we will discuss soft skills and their importance to women to excel as leaders.

What are Soft Skills?

Soft skills are the skills, abilities, and traits about your personality, attitude, and behavior. There are several skills that collectively constitute soft skills such as self-management skills, communication skills, speaking skills, writing skills, reading skills, listening skills, leadership skills, teambuilding skills, decision-making skills, conflict-management skills, problem solving skills, time management skills, career management skills, critical thinking skills, customer service skills, negotiation skills, networking skills, entrepreneurial skills, analytical skills, interpersonal skills, emotional intelligence and initiative to name a few.

Soft Skills versus Hard Skills

"With hard skills, you can manage your boss; and with soft skills, you can lead your boss." —Professor M.S. Rao

Soft skills are different from hard skills because hard skills are all about technical skills which are also known as domain skills. Therefore, soft skills are non-domain skills and also known as people skills and interpersonal skills. Soft skills are the polite and pleasing way of communicating with others, whereas hard skills are what you contribute in the workplace. Soft skills complement your hard skills. Succinctly, soft skills are the presentation of your hard skills in the workplace. Soft skills are interpersonal skills, whereas hard skills are job-related skills. Soft skills help execute domain activities effectively and efficiently. A judicious blend of both soft and hard skills are essential to achieving professional and career success. The significance of soft skills is felt more in the senior level positions as senior-level leaders focus less on hard skills but more on soft skills such as strategic planning, visioning, and trouble-shooting skills.

The significance of Soft Skills

Soft skills encourage people to come together in pursuit of shared goals in the organizations. They help women become successful and excel as entrepreneurs. Globally there is more significance attached to soft skills in information and communication services; professional, scientific and technical services; business administration and support services and financial services.

Lack of soft skills adversely affects individuals and organizations. Most hiring managers say that soft skills are 'difficult' to find in job aspirants. In the future, several workers will be held back by the lack of soft skills. Hence, there must be an initiative from all quarters to equip soft skills for men and women to improve organizational bottom lines.

Both soft and hard skills are essential for organizations to achieve their goals and objectives. Given the choice between the two, it is soft skills that are more important than hard skills. It is easy to teach hard skills but tough to train soft skills to employees. Hence, if organizations find employees with soft skills, they must retain and engage them effectively to improve the bottom lines.

Women chief executives are often found to be not getting along with the board members leading to their exit. Having soft skills helps them get along well with the board members and stakeholders to excel as successful CEOs.

How to Improve Your Soft Skills?

"Knowing is not enough; we must apply. Willing is not enough; we must do." —Johann Wolfgang von Goethe

You can acquire soft skills through various means including observation, reading, training, experience, and practice. Soft skills training equips you with skills, abilities, and knowledge. However, your interaction with others helps acquire soft skills greatly. Since soft skills are behavioral skills, people must learn by trial and error by using their emotional intelligence, and through flexibility and adaptability. You must be practical, realistic, and situational to acquire soft skills. Above all, you must learn from your failures to improve your behavior to get along well with others effectively.

You must develop emotional intelligence and interpersonal skills. You must observe and understand people and their behaviors. Travel unknown destinations to understand people. Talk to them to get along with them. Understand their cultures and behaviors. Traveling teaches tolerance and improves soft skills. When you travel to unknown destinations and communicate in a non-native language, you will be able to improve soft skills effectively.

Reading soft skills is one aspect and applying them is another aspect. Attending workshops and training programs help you understand what really are soft skills and how you will be able to acquire them because such programs conduct role-plays to bring out behavioral improvement. Here are some tools and techniques to improve soft skills

- Be self-aware.
- Avoid pre-conceived notions.
- Adopt the mirroring technique to connect with the speaker.
- Pay attention to the speaker with your positive body language. Don't offer your judgment during the conversation.
- Maintain eye contact with the speaker. Show authenticity while listening to the speaker.
- Empathize with the speaker.
- Identify a few positive traits in the speaker and appreciate to build chemistry during the conversation.
- Avoid interrupting the speaker. Respect time. Share the authentic information and make your conversation interesting and inspiring.
- Be assertive and tactful. Avoid cutting short the conversation abruptly.
- Be flexible.
- Avoid using the words 'always' and 'never.'
- Oppose ideas, not individuals.
- Accept criticism graciously.
- Praise publicly and criticize privately.
- Interact with different types of personalities who are introvert, extrovert, assertive, submissive, and aggressive.
- Stay calm, cool and composed during conversations. If the conversation is leading to arguments, exit politely and smoothly.
- Above all, be adaptable.

Since soft skills are behavioral skills, you can acquire soft skills through physical interaction and trial and error. You must take intrapersonal and interpersonal feedback regularly to improve soft skills. Succinctly, be proactive, be a good listener, improve interpersonal skills and build relationships to acquire soft skills.

> Women who get soft skills training wind up staying in the entrepreneurship or business development programs for longer, feel more successful and keep pursuing the small business path.

Conclusion

"In today's competitive environment, it is not enough to be the best in your field, intellectually. Competency is only half of what you need to climb the ladder of success. The other half is the softer side of you – it's that part of you that will be liked, admired, trusted and remembered." —Carole Nicola Ides

The dearth of soft skills will adversely affect accommodation, food services, retail, health and social work sectors in the future. Therefore, there must be coordinated and integrated efforts from all stakeholders including individuals, organizations, intellectuals, educational institutions, policy-makers, thought leaders, government and nonprofits to promote soft skills in all spheres.

"The way hard and soft skills are essential to achieving your career success, 'what you know' and 'whom you know' are essential to fast-track your career." —Professor M.S. Rao

References

https://www.amazon.com/Soft-Skills-Overcome-Workplace-Challenges/dp/1628653035

https://www.emeraldinsight.com/doi/full/10.1108/OTH-06-2017-0034 https://www.allthingsic.com/wp-content/uploads/2015/01/The-Value-of-Soft-Skills-to-the-UK-Economy.pdf

https://www.adeccogroup.com/wp-content/themes/ado-group/downloads/the-adecco-group-white-paper-the-soft-skills-imperative.pdf

Soft Skills: Your Step-by-Step Guide to Overcome Workplace Challenges to Excel as a Leader by Prof M S Rao (Motivational Press, Inc. 2016)

10 – NETWORKING SKILLS FOR WOMEN LEADERS

"You can make more friends in two months by becoming interested in other people than you can in two years by trying to get other people interested in you." —Dale Carnegie

It is not *what* you know but *who*m you know matters in this networked world. Having connections helps you greatly to fast-track your career. Some people get quick visibility while some remain incognito forever. Some people even leave this world as unsung heroes and heroines. Therefore, having connections helps you greatly to achieve success. In this chapter, we will discuss the importance of networking skills for women leaders.

What is Networking?

"Networking is marketing. Marketing yourself, marketing your uniqueness, marketing what you stand for." —Christine Comaford-Lynch

Some people perceive networking negatively. In fact, networking is to help others and seek help from others to achieve personal, professional and social goals. It is to add value to others. Michele Jennae remarked, "Networking is not about just connecting people. It's about connecting people with people, people with ideas, and people with opportunities." Hence, people must develop a positive perception of networking.

LeanIn.Org and McKinsey & Company[1] found in their major new study—with almost 30,000 employees across 118 companies that women's odds of advancement are 15% lower than men's. A study[2] explains "Women and men agree that sponsorship is vital to success and advancement, with two-thirds describing it as "very" or "extremely" important. Yet they do not have the same type of professional networks, which may result in different levels of support." It is obvious from these research findings that women lack strong networking skills socially, professionally and virtually. Hence, they receive the news of employment opportunities much later than men. In fact, most employment opportunities are not available through newspaper advertisements. They are filled mostly through connections and referral recruitments. The people who work in the companies know about the openings and refer their close connections who get shortlisted and selected. The incentives are directly credited into the accounts of the people who referred the candidates. It is obvious that things have changed from the conventional methods of recruitment to advanced methods of recruitment. People who know the top people can get access to opportunities for employment. After joining the organizations, the employees who have strong connections with the top hierarchy in the organizations get promoted quickly.

3Cs—Content, Communication and Connections

"A really important part of networking is actually about what you bring to the table-not just what you want to get out of it. The contribution is a big part of networking success." —Gina Romero

Currently, 3Cs are essential to succeed in all spheres—content, communication, and connections. Content is king while

---

1 https://www.mckinsey.com/featured-insights/gender-equality/women-in-the-workplace-2017

2 https://www.huffingtonpost.com/marilyn-nagel/women-network-differently_b_8259538.html

communication is queen. When your content is strong, you earn respect from others. At the same time, you must have strong communication skills to convey your content to reach the right audiences. Connections are the people who spread a word about your content and communication. Hence, having content, communication, and connections helps you achieve amazing success in all spheres.

Tips for Women to Network with Others

"It's great to spend time at a networking event with someone you know and like. But that's not what you're there for. Your goal is to expand your network by meeting new people." —Beth Ramsay

Networking is an art, not rocket science. Anybody can network if he or she acquire basic tools and techniques. Here are some tools for women to network with others successfully.

Women must diversify network development strategies. They must treat other women as allies, not enemies to build strong networks. They must network with both women and men equally. They must not seek favors immediately. They must extend their hands and explore opportunities. Currently, there is more of 'boys club' than 'girls club' in the organizations. Hence, they must network with both clubs to advance their careers.

Whenever you get an opportunity, seize it to deliver a speech to get noticed. You must come forward to deliver the talks during public events, functions and award ceremonies. It enhances your visibility and offers innumerable opportunities. Remember to emphasize quality connections. Instead of networking with too many people, choose a few people especially 2-3 people with positive body language in the events and talk to them. Exchange business cards with them. Follow-up. Note down their email ids and send them an email with a thank-you note. In case, if there are any opportunities, your email helps them connect back with you. In a nutshell, to be a successful networker, you must be an attentive listener, empathize with others, emotionally intelligent, ask the right questions, respect the listener, add value to the listener and make a difference.

> In PricewaterhouseCoopers' 2016 "Women in the Workplace" report[3], the study found that men were more networked with other men than women were. That may be obvious, but they worked out the math:
>
> Men: 37 percent networked mostly with other men; nine percent, mostly women; 55 percent, equal split
>
> Women: 27 percent networked mostly with other women; 27 percent, mostly men; 45 percent, equal split
>
> Because the upper echelons of organizations are overwhelmingly male, this means that fewer women are networked with the people who can introduce them into these areas. While it may seem self-explanatory, this concept of strategic networking is profoundly important for women.

Networking in the Internet World

"Networking is an investment in your business. It takes time and when done correctly can yield great results for years to come." — Diane Helbig

Internet and technology have thrown tremendous opportunities for ordinary individuals to excel as extraordinary individuals. If people know how to create original content and share it with their audiences on social media with right hashtags at the right time, they can be seen easily and promoted quickly. There are ordinary people who showcase their skills, knowledge, abilities, and talents through YouTube channel and get recognition instantly. They build networks and create a fan base. They build their leadership brands.

---

3   https://www.entrepreneur.com/article/305542

Conclusion

"Networking is about making meaningful, lasting connections that lead to one-to-one relationships." —Les Garnas

If a raindrop falls into an ocean, it loses its significance; if the same raindrop falls into a shell, it becomes a pearl. It is obvious that the right people must connect with the right people at the right time to achieve the right outcomes. The difference between the lucky people and the unlucky people is that the lucky people have connections while the unlucky people don't have any connections. To conclude, network with others and add value to them to fast-track your career and build your leadership brand globally.

"Make a list of 200 prestigious, influential, and powerful people with whom you want to work, play, grow and do business." —Mark Victor Hansen

References

https://www.mckinsey.com/featured-insights/gender-equality/women-in-the-workplace-2017

https://www.huffingtonpost.com/marilyn-nagel/women-network-differently_b_8259538.html

https://www.entrepreneur.com/article/305542

11 – Close the Gender Pay Gap Globally

"Employers must make far-reaching changes to employment terms and conditions for women: Equal pay for equal, decent work." —Phumzile Mlambo-Ngcuka

Globally gender pay gap is a burning topic but a very few take it seriously to bridge the gap earnestly. If women are equipped with negotiation skills the gender pay gap can be minimized in organizations. In fact, women find it hard to negotiate their salary. They are behind men in expressing and expecting the desired outcomes in salary and compensation. In this chapter, we will discuss negotiation skills for women and the methods they must adopt to negotiate their salary, seek compensation and ask for a raise successfully.

Gender Differences in Negotiations

"During a negotiation, it would be wise not to take anything personally. If you leave personalities out of it, you will be able to see opportunities more objectively." —Brian Koslow

Women must learn how to negotiate their salaries to end up rich at the end of their careers. Failing to do so will result in undervaluing their resumes, low productivity and low morale in the workplace. They must remember that unless they ask, they don't get what they want. While negotiating pay compensation men are direct and women are indirect in their approaches. At times it becomes difficult for employers to understand what women want. Therefore, women must communicate clearly about their expectations. Sheryl Sandberg remarked, "If you are negotiating for a raise and you are a man, you can walk in and say 'I deserve this.' That will not backfire on you. We know the data says it will backfire on a woman. So, I think along with saying 'I deserve this', explaining that this is important for your performance, and this will make you more effective as a team member."

Women must remember that gender stereotypes are pervasive. They are often at a disadvantage position at the negotiation table thus adversely impacting negotiations. Hence, they must ask what they want during negotiations. They must not react negatively across the negotiating table. They must maintain neutral body language; avoid expressing eagerness to get employment or overexcitement if offered more salary; keep cool and composed. They must focus on their core skills and strengths and bargain from the position of strength.

Make Your Negotiation a "Win-Win"

"This is a classic negotiation technique. It's a gentle, soft indication of your disapproval and a great way to keep negotiating. Count to 10. By then, the other person usually will start talking and may very well make a higher offer." —Bill Coleman

Salary negotiation is a collaborative process between the employer and the employee. It must be a win-win outcome to ensure employee engagement effectively and achieve organizational excellence and effectiveness.

Be realistic when you negotiate your salary. Do research to find out the prevailing salaries paid in your current position in your industry. Ask for a reasonable hike. Don't quote sky high as you lose the chances of getting an employment offer. Fix low and high figures on your mind and negotiate to make it win-win. A win-win outcome is always better than a lose-win or win-lose outcome. If you are convinced that others are getting salaries better than you, be assertive to ask for it. If you find that the present employer doesn't pay as your abilities, explore employment opportunities elsewhere to get a higher salary. When you know your true worth and the prevailing salaries in your industry, you can negotiate from a position of strength.

> The World Economic Forum[1] said it would take 217 years for disparities in the pay and employment opportunities of men and women to end.

Initiatives to Close the Gender Pay Gap Globally

"Women have fought long and hard for a seat at the table. My role at PepsiCo is a testament to the strides we've made. Yet as women enter the workforce in larger numbers than ever before, new challenges emerge. We need to eliminate a wage gap that has women around the world earning the same amount men did roughly a decade ago. We need to empower women by providing them with the support they need to do their jobs and care for their families — because no one should have to choose between his or her career aspirations and those they love. I'm fighting for gender parity because businesses thrive when we open the doors of opportunity to extraordinary women, and societies thrive whenever and wherever we can unlock the potential of all our people, women and men alike." — Indra Nooyi, Ex-CEO, PepsiCo

Countries including Iceland, Norway, Finland, Sweden, and Denmark have taken appropriate measures to close the gender pay gap. For instance, Iceland fines for companies with gender wage gaps; Norway pays mandatory paternal leave; Finland and Sweden offer flexible schedules; and Denmark provides partially-subsidized and affordable childcare. Shelley Zalis in her Forbes article, *Lessons From The World's Most Gender-Equal Countries* unveils, "Iceland[2] has

---

1   https://www.theguardian.com/society/2017/nov/01/gender-pay-gap-217-years-to-close-world-economic-forum

2   https://www.forbes.com/sites/shelleyzalis/2018/10/30/lessons-from-the-worlds-most-gender-equal-countries/#376cab727dd8

become the first country in the world to make the gender pay gap illegal, with a new law requiring companies with 25 or more employees to prove that they pay men and women equally for equal work."

Global companies including Starbucks, Intel, Salesforce.com, GoDaddy and Accenture have taken the right steps to bridge the gender pay gap. Selena Rezvani[3] writes in her article, *Six Companies Hacking The Gender Wage Gap*, "A new study shows that a full 80% of women would leave a company for one that offered better gender equality. The same study highlights that an additional 78% of respondents say a workplace where people are treated equally — regardless of gender, sexual orientation, age, race or religion — is important to them. And yet, roughly half of female workers (56%) and male workers (52%) surveyed believe their employers could do more to promote gender equality and diversity." She suggests minimizing salary histories; setting promotion parity targets; using promotion flagging; taking a hard line; and amplifying the message.

The Colombian native, Sofia Vergara continues to reign as the queen of TV. She is the highest paid actress on the small screen for the seventh year in a row, quadrupling her income from the previous year. What makes TV different from the movie world is that the gender pay gap is considerably less in television. While in movies, male stars frequently pocket a lot more than their female counterparts, TV has a far smaller gap between actors and actresses, at least among top earners.

Conclusion

"A negotiator should observe everything. You must be part Sherlock Holmes, part Sigmund Freud." —Victor Kiam

Salaries must be paid as per the competence, experience, knowledge, skills and abilities, not based on gender. It is a well-admitted fact that salaries are not same even for men because salaries are paid as per the prevailing demand and supply in the market and

---

3   https://www.forbes.com/sites/selenarezvani1/2018/04/13/
    six-companies-hacking-the-gender-wage-gap/#5dc8075f7055

based on their performance. To conclude, pay equality is an issue between the genders. If leaders are serious, global organizations can reduce the pay gap by 2040.

"We need to stop buying into the myth about gender equality. It isn't a reality yet. Today, women make up half of the U.S. workforce, but the average working woman earns only 77 percent of what the average working man makes. But unless women and men both say this is unacceptable, things will not change. Men have to demand that their wives, daughters, mothers, and sisters earn more—commensurate with their qualifications and not their gender. Equality will be achieved when men and women are granted equal pay and equal respect." — Beyoncé, Singer

References

https://www.theguardian.com/society/2017/nov/01/gender-pay-gap-217-years-to-close-world-economic-forum

https://www.forbes.com/sites/shelleyzalis/2018/10/30/lessons-from-the-worlds-most-gender-equal-countries/#376cab727dd8

https://www.forbes.com/sites/selenarezvani1/2018/04/13/six-companies-hacking-the-gender-wage-gap/#5dc8075f7055

https://www.usatoday.com/story/life/tv/2018/10/25/highest-paid-tv-actress-sofia-vergara-tops-list/1765520002/

12 – Women Cannot Have it All

"Being in control of your life and having realistic expectations about your day-to-day challenges are the keys to stress management, which is perhaps the most important ingredient to living a happy, healthy and rewarding life."
—Marilu Henner

Indra Nooyi said brutally in her interview with *The Atlantic*, "I don't think women can have it all. I just don't think so. We pretend we have it all. We pretend we can have it all." She added, "You die with guilt. You just die with guilt. My observation is that the biological clock and the career clock are in total conflict with each other. Total, complete conflict. When you have to have kids you have to build your career. Just as you're rising to middle management your kids need you because they're teenagers."

The fact is that nobody can have it all. There is no point in highlighting it from a gender perspective. We must learn to live with realities and balance personal, professional and social life as far as possible to provide meaning to our lives. Hence, Indra Nooyi's statement doesn't have any substance and it doesn't inspire women in any way. She could not balance her professional and personal life that doesn't mean other women cannot balance. When you look at women leaders including Diane Sawyer, Martha Stewart, Estee Lauder, Ruth Hamdler, Debbi Fields, and Arianna Huffington, they have it all. Hence, it is obvious that Indra Nooyi is not an ideal example of work-life balance. When you look at American President,

Barack Obama, he maintains work-life balance. He spends a considerable amount of time with his family.

People have their own expectations and work toward achieving them. But life takes its own twists and turns and finally, people land somewhere else. We propose something and God disposes of something else. Life is not a cakewalk. We work hard to achieve something and the outcomes are beyond our control.

Challenges for Women

"You've got to keep women in the workforce, whether it's through having children, caring for elder parents, all the things. Not that husbands, spouses, and partners don't do those things as well, but it's often what takes them out, and then to get them back in is hard. You keep them in the workforce and your odds are much higher. And that's one of the many things we do (at IBM)" —Ginni Rometty, CEO, Chairman and President of IBM

Women undergo lots of challenges at home and office. They have professional roles and responsibilities at the office. They must manage office politics. Sometimes, they face sexual harassment in the workplace. After reaching home, they must manage their husbands, children, and parents. It is a tough job indeed! Bill George advised, "To lead an integrated life, you need to bring together the major elements of your personal life and professional life, including work, community, and friends, so that you can be the same person in each environment."

Some women refuse to accept senior positions because of several reasons including caregiving responsibilities at home, commuting long distances, attending events, traveling and elderly parents with medical issues.

Work-Life Balance for Women

"We're so engaged in doing things to achieve purposes of outer value that we forget that the inner value – the rapture that is associated with being alive – is what it is all about." —Joseph Campbell

Work-life balance is a challenging issue for both men and women. In fact, it is more challenging for women as they must take a break for their motherhood and take care of their children at home. Currently, employees work very hard to earn their livelihood and beat the competition. Hence, taking care of all aspects is not an easy thing. If anybody has it all, he or she is truly blessed.

For women, there is often a conflict between the biological clock and career clock. Balancing both is a challenging task for them. Companies including Facebook and Google encourage work-life integration which gives some leisure time for their employees to pursue their hobbies or to relax during the working hours to enable them to recharge.

Instead of searching for work-life balance, women must reframe their mind and integrate work and life to lead a complete life. Previously people worked hard for more than 8 hours a day for 6 days a week. Presently people work smart for 8 hours a day for 5 days a week. In the future, people will work wise 6 hours a day for 4 days a week. Therefore, we are looking forward to a world where people have the cake and eat it too. That means, they enjoy during work hours and achieve peak performance in the workplace.

Conclusion

"I don't think women can have it all. I just don't think so. We pretend we have it all. We pretend we can have it all. My husband and I have been married for 34 years. And we have two daughters. And every day you have to make a decision about whether you are going to be a wife or a mother, in fact, many times during the day you have to make those decisions. And you have to co-opt a lot of people to help you. We co-opted our families to help us. We plan our lives meticulously so we can be decent parents. But if you ask our daughters, I'm not sure they will say that I've been a good mom. I'm not sure. And I try all kinds of coping mechanisms." —Indra Nooyi

The solution lies in not comparing with others. Women must not compare with other women in businesses, careers, children, money, and jewelry. To conclude, it is not possible for both men and women to have it all. Especially for leaders and C-suite executives, it is tough to manage their time and juggle their roles and responsibilities from time to time.

"Life is indeed beautiful. It's times when we sink into our hectic and stressful lifestyles that we are blinded and fail to see what we really have." —Unknown

13 – ADVOCATE #MeToo MOVEMENT

"Man is born to a woman—and if he doesn't respect women, he manifestly lacks understanding of his very existence." — Professor M.S. Rao

Finally, the world has woken up with #MeToo movement with several women breaking their silence and accusing men of sexual harassment and sexual assault. It is a great movement globally to ensure dignity and honor of women. When the victims leveled sexual harassment charges in the past, courts and corporates addressed them earnestly. With #MeToo movement, victims can come out openly both online and offline to speak against the tormentors, perpetrators, and predators who abused them.

#MeToo Movement

"I founded the Me Too Movement because there was a void in the community that I was in. There were gaps in services. There was dearth in resources, and I saw young people – I saw black and brown girls – who are hurting and who needed something that just wasn't there." —Tarana Burke

It was Tarana Burke, a black activist who founded the #MeToo movement in 2006. She said, "'Me Too' is about letting – using the power of empathy to stomp out shame." With the rapid growth in technology especially social media, the movement gained attention quickly. There is a difference between #MeToo movement and sexual harassment. The Society for Human Resource Management[1] defines sexual harassment as, "Unwelcome conduct of a sexual nature that is sufficiently persistent or offensive to unreasonably interfere with an employee's job performance or create an intimidating, hostile or offensive working environment." And International Labour Organisation (ILO) defines sexual harassment as unwelcome sexual advances or verbal or physical conduct of a sexual nature that has the effect of unreasonably interfering with an individual's work performance or creating an intimidating, hostile, abusive or offensive working environment. It is obvious that sexual harassment is a subset of #MeToo movement.

#MeToo movement can be defined as the movement where the victims can voice publicly about sexual misconduct, sexual harassment, sexual assault, horrors, and rape against predators, perpetrators, and tormentors to bring culprits to book. It is neither a social media steroid nor a publicity stunt. It is not a male bashing but to ensure safe workplaces and societies for both men and women. Fortunately, social media has become a boon for harassed men and women to share their stories of harassment, horrors, sexual assault and rape from perpetrators and predators. Here are some facts and cautions about #MeToo movement.

- #MeToo movement is not only for women but also for men. Hence, men must also come out openly against women who harassed them and abused them sexually.
- #MeToo movement is not meant for settling your personal scores in public places. It is to book the culprits and bring justice for both men and women who have been abused in the past.
- #MeToo movement is not a platform to kick up controversy and build your brand. It is to speak about the harassment in the past and take legal action against the abusers.

---

1   https://www.shrm.org/resourcesandtools/tools-and-samples/poli-
cies/pages/cms_000554.aspx

- Don't exploit social media to settle your personal scores in public places. Maintain ethics and etiquette. Complain with facts and figures. Take legal action to get justice. Remember that truth alone triumphs at the end.
- Ensure that #MeToo movement doesn't widen the gap between men and women.

Steps to Prevent Sexual Harassment in the Workplace

"I don't think that every single case of sexual harassment has to result in someone being fired; the consequences should vary. But we need a shift in culture so that every single instance of sexual harassment is investigated and dealt with. That's just basic common sense." —Tarana Burke

One of the main advantages of #MeToo movement is that the office romance has come down drastically as employees are scared about its misuse by others to settle their personal scores. Previously office politics were confined to the office alone. Now they have hit the social media platforms. Consider the following tips to avoid getting into sexual harassment cases in the workplace.

- Be assertive while handling your colleagues, superiors, and subordinates.
- Avoid excessive socialization in the workplace.
- Avoid inappropriate behavior in the workplace such as unwanted touching and comments especially others' dress code and style.
- Avoid sexually explicit forwards on social media and WhatsApp.
- Don't stare at a person for more than five seconds.
- Be professional and stick to office ethics and etiquette; and roles and responsibilities.
- Keep cultural aspects in view when you work in a global environment because what might appear as normal for one individual may appear as sexual harassment for another individual.

- Gifting is a great habit. Ensure that the recipient doesn't view it negatively in the workplace.
- Understand the difference between intentions and actions; and intent and impact. At times, it is the impact rather than the intent that constitutes sexual harassment.
- Avoid conversations with difficult individuals and jerks.
- Behave carefully as the relationships are dynamic in the workplace with changing equations and challenges.
- Use your head, not heart when you associate with your colleagues especially opposite sex or with the same sex if you are a gay or a lesbian.
- Draw a clear line between your professional responsibilities and personal relations in the workplace. Don't interfere excessively into others' personal issues and don't allow them to enter into your personal issues.

Organizations must provide anti-harassment training to educate employees about the dos and don'ts in the workplace. They must educate employees about the activities and behaviors that fall under the bracket of sexual harassment. They must strengthen their existing laws to prevent sexual harassment and abuses in the workplace. Adequate care must be taken before firing the accused employees. Apart from rules and regulations, there must be a change in the mindset of the people to respect diversity and inclusion.

At a time when the fake information goes viral much faster than the factual information, it is essential to ensure the sanctity of the #MeToo movement by checking the accusations for accuracy and authenticity. The investigators must be unbiased and professional. They must check whether the claims are credible. They must check the facts before coming to the conclusion. They must check whether the allegations have been made to settle their personal scores in a professional environment and public places.

Conclusion

"'Me too' was just two words; it's two magic words that galvanized the world." —Tarana Burke

So far, MeToo has remained as an elitist movement. It must reach average and ordinary individuals to enable them to come out openly and boldly to punish the culprits. It is essential to sustain this movement in the larger interests of society.

#MeToo movement is neither a male bashing nor a female bashing. It is neither a social media steroid nor a publicity stunt. It is the voice of the victims that was suppressed for many years. It is a cry of the women and men who have been harassed and abused. It must be taken seriously and addressed earnestly. It must be welcomed wholeheartedly to build better societies globally. If we want to survive as a healthy civilization advocating this movement is essential. To conclude, #MeToo movement helps advance women empowerment and achieve gender equality globally. Hence, everyone must welcome this movement irrespective of his or her gender to ensure dignity and honor for both sexes.

"I think women are foolish to pretend they are equal to men. They are far superior and always have been. Whatever you give a woman, she will make greater. If you give her sperm, she'll give you a baby. If you give her a house, she'll give you a home. If you give her groceries, she'll give you a meal. If you give her a smile, she'll give you her heart. She multiplies and enlarges what is given to her. So, if you give her any crap, be prepared to receive a ton of shit!"
—Sir William Golding

There appears to be a disconnect between men's interest in gender diversity and their understanding of the challenges women face: 70 percent think gender diversity is important, but only 12 percent believe women have fewer opportunities.

References

https://www.thepeoplespace.com/ideas/articles/how-metoo-helps-prevent-sexual-harassment-workplace
https://www.shrm.org/resourcesandtools/tools-and-samples/policies/pages/cms_000554.aspx

14 – THE MIND OF A WOMAN CEO

"The most important factor in determining whether you will succeed isn't your gender, it's you. Be open to opportunity and take risks. In fact, take the worst, the messiest, the most challenging assignment that you can find, and then take control." —Angela Braly

Do you think CEOs are a breed apart? Do you think the minds of the CEOs are unconventional? Do you think the minds of the women CEOs unique? You can explore answers for them in this chapter.

The minds of the CEOs must be a blend of various skills, abilities, knowledge, education, and experience. The CEOs must be great listeners, learners, leaders, and troubleshooters. They must be resilient and visionaries with a laser focus approach toward execution. They must aim at hitting the bull's eye. They must be brave, original thinkers, fast-paced and engage all stakeholders effectively to accomplish organizational goals and objectives. They must be driven, resilient, team builders and effective communicators. They must be risk takers, persuasive, competitive and above all, aggressive in executing their vision. They must possess soft skills, hard skills, conceptual skills, and emotional intelligence quotient. They must have a transformational mindset without compromising the transactional mindset. They must be soft leaders, not hard leaders. They must be prepared mentally to overcome obstacles and challenges effectively. They must not follow standard tools and techniques because what worked in the past may now work now and what works now may not work in the future. They must lead all the stakeholders including customers, employees, financial institutions, government bodies, board members and the media successfully. Precisely, they must be ordinary executives with an extraordinary mindset, tool-set, and skillset.

Undoubtedly, CEOs are a breed apart from others. However, everyone can aspire to reach C-level positions if he or she adopts the right tools and techniques in the early stage of his or her careers. Dr. Susan Madsen, Professor of Leadership & Ethics, Utah Valley University rightly remarked, "Leaders are not just born. Sure, some people are born with strong competencies and strengths for leading in certain situations, but it is very clear that leadership can also be developed. That means everyone can strengthen their skills and abilities to lead and influence."

Steps for Women to Reach CEO Positions

"You need to have more women like me or others that say, 'We did it, so you can

do it too.' That, to me, is probably the most important thing to do. The second big thing is that you need to involve the men because if we think we're going to go it alone, it's not going to happen." —Monica Mandelli

Research shows that women often don't use their full potential due to cultural and gender aspects. Before aspiring for senior positions, women must put their hands on their hearts and ask themselves whether they are using their potential fully.

It is a well-admitted fact that women care for others. Men buy for themselves while women buy for their spouses, children, and parents. If you want your organization to achieve excellence and effectiveness you must hire women with passion and potential and groom them in their initial stage of careers. Here are a few steps to ensure more women reaching C-level positions especially CEO position.

- Create opportunities for women at all levels.
- Inspire them to overcome their inhibitions.

- Encourage them to participate actively in cross-functional roles and responsibilities. Adopt job rotation.
- Assign cross-training roles and responsibilities to enable them to become the jack of all trades and master of their domains.

Most people strongly opine that men are natural leaders because they have leadership skills inherently. It is a myth indeed! Additionally, there is a stereotypic bias that prevents women from reaching the top positions. Hence, organizations must address the impact of stereotypic bias to enable the women talent to excel.

> Men's success can be attributed to their skills while women's success can be attributed to their efforts and luck. Men's failure can be attributed to their bad luck while women's failure can be attributed to their inability. It is essential to break such stereotypes.

Conclusion

"What I wanted was to be allowed to do the thing in the world that I did best—which I believed then and believe now is the greatest privilege there is. When I did that, success found me." —Debbi Fields

Closing the gender gap is the key to corporate excellence and effectiveness. Currently, the pipeline for women is leaking with the reports of women CEOs stepping down globally. It must be checked to ensure a seamless supply of women CEOs to lead global organizations.

The present corporate world is designed by men which are laying the ladder for women leaders to reach C-level positions slowly. Therefore, we must allow women to design their ladder in the corporate world to enable them to fast-track their careers. If appropriate measures are taken now, it will take approximately 30 years to bridge the gender gap to reach CEOs positions.

Hopefully, we will ensure more women leaders reaching C-suite positions by 2050.

"If you are committed to creating value and if you aren't afraid of hard times, obstacles become utterly unimportant. A nuisance perhaps, but with no real power. The world respects creation; people will get out of your way." —Candice Carpenter

15 – Think Crisis; Think Woman

"20% of the world's data is searchable. Anybody can get to that 20%. But 80% of the world's data is where I think the real gold is, whether its decades of underwriting, pricing, customer experience, risk in loans – that is all with our clients. You don't want to share it. That is gold." —Virginia M. Rometty, *Chairman, President, and Chief Executive Officer, IBM*

When you look at CEOs including Ginni Rometty of IBM, Mary Barra of General Motors, Craig Weatherup, of PepsiCo, David Neeleman of JetBlue and James E. Burke of Johnson & Johnson; they overcame crises successfully. When you look at inspiring leaders including Sheryl Sandberg, COO of Facebook; Angela Merkel, Chancellor of Germany; Janet Yellen, Chairwoman of the Federal Reserve Bank; Susan Wojcicki, CEO of YouTube; Queen Victoria of England; Margaret Thatcher, the first female Prime Minister of Britain; Golda Meir, the first female prime minister of Israel; they overcame several odds to establish as successful women leaders globally.

Research shows that the companies helmed by women leaders overcame organizational crises successfully. Companies believe that women can work under pressure to turnaround ailing organizations. However, psychology professors Michelle Ryan and Alex Haslam call it 'glass cliff' where women are more likely to be put into leadership roles and responsibilities. Whatever the term is used, it is a fact that women can handle crises effectively. In this regard, we will discuss Ginni Rometty's leadership style and her ability to keep IBM on the growth track successfully.

IBM survived several crises throughout its history and bounced back from several challenges to stay relevant, competent and successful in corporate history. Various CEOs have adopted leadership tools and techniques to turnaround, and grow their companies based on their mindsets and leadership principles and philosophies. The challenges were different, and the way they handled them was also different. Lou Gerstner turned around IBM. John Spence in his book, *Awesomely Simple: Essential Business Strategies for Turning Ideas Into Action* shares about turning around IBM as follows: Lou Gerstner, who, ironically, took over as the new CEO on April Fools' Day in 1993, is straightforward and clear: completely changing the culture toward transparency, teamwork, customer focus, and extremely fast action. From his study of the situation and personal experience working inside the company, it seems to him that the turnaround was based on four major strategies:

1. Create strong, collaborative partnerships with customers, and sustain an intense focus on the marketplace.
2. Drive unique value and growth through innovation and offering value-added solutions rather than products.
3. Invest heavily in finding, keeping, and developing the best people, and keep them focused on furthering core competencies.
4. Leverage the skills and knowledge of those people through collaboration, communication, teamwork, and a strong sense of urgency.

How did this work for IBM? Between 1991 and 1993, IBM lost a breathtaking $16 billion. In what was termed the most remarkable turnaround of any company ever, IBM reported a net income of $7.58 billion on revenues of $89.13 billion ten years later, in 2003. The ideas that Lou Gerstner used to turnaround one of the largest companies on the face of the earth are not complex; they merely require focused effort and disciplined execution.

Sam Palmisano took IBM from good to great with his leadership style by overcoming several leadership challenges. For instance, at the height of the dot-com bust in 2002, he acquired the consulting arm of the accounting firm PricewaterhouseCoopers and stepped up investments in R&D which was considered a wrong move. But he proved his critics wrong by leading from the front with his business and technical acumen. He invested his capital into businesses with high returns to improve the organizational bottom lines. He bought small companies that paid high returns. He compressed working capital to get more returns.

Think Crisis; Think Woman

"A professional reinvention only happens if you're willing to do stuff that makes you squirm." —Suzy Welch

Ginni Rometty took over as IBM's CEO on Oct. 1, 2012, from Sam Palmisano when the company was encountering an existential crisis as rapidly rising cloud computing technology threatened its core businesses. She successfully brought it to good shape with her vast experience and expertise. Although some of her decisions were questioned such as selling semiconductor manufacturing operations of IBM, she proved her critics wrong with her daring decisions and amazing performance.

According to the 2016 BNP Paribas Global Entrepreneur Report[1], companies helmed by female entrepreneurs had 13% higher revenues than those run by men and finished 9% above the average.

---

1   http://fortune.com/2016/02/29/women-entrepreneurs-success/

Ginni Rometty—A Turnaround Heroin

"Today, IBM is much more than a "hardware, software, services" company. IBM is now emerging as a cognitive solutions and cloud platform company." —Virginia M. Rometty

Ginni Rometty is the first female head of the IBM. She rose through the ranks in a number of leadership roles since 1981. She is workaholic, courageous and teambuilder. She takes risks and knows how to inspire her team to achieve organizational goals and objectives. She asserts that comfort and growth never co-exist. She implores that women employees must be judged on the basis of their work and not on ethnicity, religion or sexual orientation. She remarked, "The lesson in my story is that please evaluate my work and then judge me. I do not want to be known as the first woman CEO of IBM. I just want to be known as the CEO of IBM." She learns from her mistakes and admits that she failed to move fast enough and take big risks in the initial stage of her career. Hence, it is essential to move to the future, make decisions from a long-term perspective and take big risks. Here are some leadership lessons from her.

- Be clear on what you believe in and about your journey.
- Be an effective communicator.
- Lead by example.
- Step out of your comfort zone.
- Take risks to succeed.
- Let go of your past.
- Engage your employees effectively.
- Take a holistic view of your customer.
- Don't shy away from shouldering responsibilities.
- Never love something so much that you can't let go of it.
- Look at everyone as a mentor. Always ask what can you take one thing away from others.
- Understand the fact that the best becomes the bar for the rest over a period of time.
- Stay inspired by role models.

- Understand the importance of data.
- Reimagine the world.

Precisely, here are the leadership lessons from her: put the client first; listen for need, envision the future; share your expertise; reinvent relentlessly; be bold to create new ideas; think, prepare and rehearse; and show personal interest.

Ginni Rometty successfully reinvented IBM as per the changing times and technologies. Under her leadership, IBM is able to compete in the fast-growing and quickly evolving healthcare industry. She has been featured in Fortune magazine's "50 Most Powerful Women in Business" for 10 consecutive years; and in the number one position for the years 2012, 2013 and 2014. She played a key role in the purchase of PricewaterhouseCoopers Consulting firm by IBM, and then later in formulating its growth strategy, and setting it into motion.

Conclusion

"I want to do it because I want to do it. Women must try to do things as men have tried. When they fail, their failure must be but a challenge to others." —Amelia Earhart

Women are often evaluated more harshly in leadership roles. Men are known as natural leaders while women are known as female leaders. Additionally, what is effective for women depends on the context in which leadership is enacted. It is clear evidence of leadership being gendered. Ginny Rometty successfully broke the stereotypes and barriers and showed to the world that women are more capable of leading organizations during crises.

"Women on the board do bring a different perspective. They think a little bit differently. They are more comfortable with ambiguity. It's not such a linear thought. Just that difference and having that give and take at the board level is very important for America's overall competitiveness." —Desiree Rogers, *former chief executive officer of Johnson Publishing Company*

References

https://www.amazon.com/21-Success-Sutras-Ceos-Rao/dp/162865290X

https://www.inc.com/john-rampton/8-historical-power-women-leaders-stories.html

https://successstory.com/people/virginia-marie-rometty

http://fortune.com/2016/02/29/women-entrepreneurs-success/

Awesomely Simple: Essential Business Strategies for Turning Ideas Into Action by John Spence (Jossey-Bass; 1 edition, September 8, 2009)

From Smart to Wise: Acting and Leading with Wisdom by Prasad Kaipa and Navi Radjou (John Wiley & Sons 16 April 2013)

16 – Strategies for Women Leaders to Excel as CEOs

"The amazing thing about IBM is that it's a company where I have had 10 different careers – local jobs, global jobs, technology jobs, industry jobs, financial services, insurance, start-ups, and big scale. The network of talent around you is phenomenal." —Ginni Rometty, *CEO, Chairman, and President of IBM.*

The women leaders must shed their inhibitions and declare their ambitions to become CEOs to get noticed in the long run. They must aim high and learn the functions of other departments to widen their knowledge base and understand the whole picture of the organization. It broadens their conceptual skills to grow as CEOs. They must build their CEO brand consistently. They must follow the concept of job rotation to excel as well-rounded professionals to become CEOs. They must possess strategic vision and knowledge. They must integrate various verticals and departments within their mind to see the big picture. They must think out-of-the-box to grow as CEOs because becoming a CEO involves leading people and troubleshooting. CEOs must think laterally and look strategically. Hence, women leaders must think laterally and act strategically to become CEOs. Since CEOs deal with various stakeholders including government agencies, financial institutions, marketing, suppliers, and clients; women leaders must set their vision in the early stage of their careers and develop the CEO mindset by learning various aspects. Here are some strategies for women leaders to reach CEO position quickly:

- **Develop a CEO Mindset:** It is rightly said that a battle is won twice—first in your mind and second in reality. You must think like a CEO first to become a CEO. Find out what is essential to become a CEO and start acquiring the knowledge, skills, and abilities to excel as a CEO.
- **Follow the Road Less Travelled:** When you look at Steve Jobs, he followed the road less traveled and excelled as an innovation legend. Hence, don't get into the rat race. Explore the unexplored areas where you find a huge potential and better opportunities, and work on them. Become a smart worker rather than a hard worker.
- **Write Your Failure Resume:** It sounds strange, right? In fact, you learn more from your failures than from others as failures teach you several hard lessons and enlighten you to analyze what did not work for you. A failure resume helps you find your blind spots. Hence, follow the three-step process while writing your failure resume. In the first column, list out your failures; in the second column, write down why you have failed; in the third column, mention what are the lessons learned from your failures. It helps you reflect your mind and serves you during introspection. Preparing a failure resume will minimize your mistakes in the future and maximize your leadership success.
- **Hone Your Conceptual Skills:** Robert Katz said that three skills are essential in varied proportions at each level of management. They are technical skills, human skills, and conceptual skills. As you reach from lower to middle and top-level management, you must possess more conceptual skills and less technical skills while the percentage of human skills remain constant at each level of management. The human skills can be called soft skills and technical skills can be called hard skills. There is an equal significance attached

to soft skills at each level of management but the significance of hard skills decreases when you reach senior-level positions as you do more of decision making and troubleshooting. In addition, you must provide your vision to your company. Hence, you must hone your conceptual skills to touch your tipping point.

- **Blend Hard and Soft Skills:** A judicious blend of hard and soft skills is essential to reach the top positions. Hard skills are about your technical aspects while soft skills are about your polite and pleasing way to communicate with others. Rather soft skills are the presentation of your hard skills. It is improper to think that hard skills alone will help you reach the top. In fact, hard skills will get you to the top while soft skills will put you firmly on your corporate ladder.

- **Emphasize EQ:** David Campbell, The Center for Creative Leadership unfolds, "Half of the CEOs in the world are below average." It is obvious that your (Emotional Quotient) EQ plays a more important role than (Intelligence Quotient) IQ. Here is the good news! EQ can be acquired through various means including reading, training, observation, experience, and practice. IQ is inborn while EQ can be cultivated. Hence, develop your EQ and blend it with IQ proportionately and effectively to reach the top.

- **Work in Teams:** When you work in teams you display your strengths and leverage others' skills. You develop tolerance to others' views and empathize with them. You also generate better results. You develop a tremendous synergy and network that will catapult you to the top quickly. Additionally, you develop emotional intelligence which is one of the key components to achieving your leadership effectiveness.

- **Be an Expert in Your Domain:** You must discover your strengths and talents and work on them. You must focus on them forever to achieve the desired outcomes quickly. Acquire knowledge continuously in your area of interest. Reinvent yourself with the changing times and technology.

Update yourself constantly by networking with the people sharing your interests, knowledge and understanding the latest developments. Build your online professional image to enable the people to appreciate your leadership brand.

- **Participate in Job Rotation:** Job rotation is about doing various tasks outside your routine nature of work. It has multiple advantages. It eliminates boredom and keeps you active. You get to know what is happening in other areas. It helps you develop conceptual skills. Above all, it helps you stay motivated. Hence, undertake various roles and responsibilities beyond your assignments within the organization to know something of everything and everything of something.

- **Build Your Leadership Brand:** Nowadays, building your brand is imperative. It is an effective tool to build your career and project your personality to others. You must be careful before branding. Choose carefully how you would like to brand yourself as your brand will enhance your professional image and ensure longevity. You must build your brand based on your principles, philosophies, competencies, and capabilities.

- **Be Loyal to Your Organization:** Some employees change their jobs often for peanuts, but they must know that changing their jobs too often adversely affects their credibility. Research shows that most CEOs worked for a long period in their organizations and ultimately, they reached the top. They emphasized their careers, not jobs. When you work in an organization for a long duration, your talents will be spotted, and you will be slotted in the leadership pipeline through continuous training and development thus reaching the top quickly. Additionally, most companies promote their senior talent for CEO position rather than hiring from outside. In fact, job hoppers took 27 years to become CEOs while the loyal ones took about 23 years to become CEOs. Hence, be loyal to your organization.

- **Embrace Change:** The only thing constant in the world is change. Hence, change before you are forced to change. Change is painful and stressful if you view it negatively. In contrast, you enjoy every moment if you view it positively and embrace it with open arms. Remember the words of Charles Darwin, "It is not the strongest of the species that survives, nor the most intelligent that survives. It is the one that is the most adaptable to change."

- **Update with the Latest Technology:** Technology is changing rapidly. You must update yourself with a rapidly changing technology to reap benefits and save your time, money and energy. In addition, most young CEOs are from the technology domain. If you are an expert in technology, do research, you will get more ideas to found your company and become a CEO in the early stage.

- **Take Feedback Regularly:** When you take feedback, you assess yourself where you stand in terms of your performance and results. If you failed to achieve your goals you will be able to identify the barriers that prevented you from accomplishing your goals. You can address them and move forward aggressively.

- **Look at Similarities, not Differences:** The globe has become a small village connecting all people together under one platform. Develop flexibility and respect all communities. Treat diversity as an opportunity, not a challenge. Be tolerant toward other communities. Empathize with others. Love your mother but don't hate another person's mother. As your mother is precious to you, another person's mother is equally precious to her. As your community is close to your heart, another person's community is equally close to her heart. Hence, look at similarities and connect with others to gain acceptance and earn respect.

- **Coach Others:** When you coach others, you earn their goodwill; develop the rapport with them; and excel as a true leader. Most employees prefer working with superiors who handhold and coach them. They look for their career guidance and support. Hence, coach people, support them and build leaders around yourself. When you do so, you stand in a better position to scale the corporate ladder quickly. Remember that real leaders build leaders around themselves.

- **Learn Continuously:** Remember the sage advice of my friend and mentor, Marshall Goldsmith, the CEO Coach, *What Got You Here Won't Get You There.* You must update yourself regularly with the latest tools and techniques to reach your next higher position. What worked to reach your present successful position might not work to reach your next higher position. Hence, acquire secrets and strategies, and update your tools and techniques to become more successful in your professional life.

"If I am not for myself, who will be for me? If I am not for others, what am I? And if not now then when?" —Hillel HaZaken

Research shows that women hold just 12% of line roles and 30% of functional roles in executive leadership teams. They make up 5% of CEOs, 9% of CFOs and 13% of Group Exec/COOs of executive leadership teams.

Reference
https://cew.org.au/wp-content/uploads/2017/09/CEW-Executive-Census-2017.pdf

17 – Build a Team of Connections Globally

"We are like islands in the sea, separate on the surface but connected in the deep." —William James

When you want to achieve an amazing success globally you must build a team of strong connections and network. After completion of your education, parents have a limited role to play in your life except in supporting your family and finance. However, when you want to fast-track your career, you must build a team of connections globally to add value to them and leverage their connections.

Advantages of Connections

"The currency of real networking is not greed but generosity." — Keith Ferrazzi

Connections are crucial for your career and leadership success. They help you keep in the right place at the right time. They help you timely and immensely. When a raindrop falls into an ocean, it loses its significance. In contrast, if the same raindrop falls into a shell, it becomes a pearl. It is obvious that right connections, coaches, and mentors help you fast-track your career. Additionally, research shows that most jobs are available based on your network rather than through advertisements.

Even if you don't have money, your connections help you greatly. That is one of the major reasons why people invest their time, energy and resources to build connections. There are people who attend events and functions to network with others. In fact, there are networking events at the end of each program to connect with like-minded people to explore opportunities. It is a well-admitted fact that behind the success of every person there is someone who laid the ladder for their success. Therefore, success is not a solo game. It is a confluence of various factors including hard work, persistence, and connections.

A 2016 study[1] from the American Economic Review found that a woman more than doubles her chances of serving on the board of a publicly traded company in Singapore if she plays golf. And while boards of directors may employ headhunters to find qualified candidates for board seats or executive positions, the roles are still often given to someone recommended by some stakeholder of the organization. At the very least, the candidate is often vouched for by "a friend of a friend."

Tools to Connect with Others

Here are some tools to build your network. Don't be shy to talk with strangers. Be comfortable to open up with them. Don't be overly conscious about making mistakes. Be cheerful. Smile to connect with others. Start your conversation based on your knowledge, skills, and abilities. Also, initiate your conversation by outlining others' areas of interest. Be a good listener first. Don't interfere when others converse with you. Present a positive body language to connect with others. Adopt the mirroring technique to connect with others quickly. Avoid interfering into their personal issues and lives. Your conversation must be professional with an emphasis on ethics and etiquette.

---

1   https://www.entrepreneur.com/article/305542

Keep your network as diverse as possible to make it powerful and inspiring. Have a strategy and execute it effectively. J. Kelly Hoey, author of *Build Your Dream Network: Forging Powerful Relationships in a Hyper-Connected World* rightly remarked, "Random outreach is not an effective approach to problem-solving; and at its core, networking really is about seeking a solution to a problem or challenge you're facing."

Add Value to Your Connections

"One of the most powerful networking practices is to provide immediate value to a new connection. This means the moment you identify a way to help someone, take action." —Lewis Howes

Instead of being a taker, you must be a giver by adding value to your connections. For instance, I help my connections globally who are mostly authors by reading and reviewing their books. They ship me books and I read and post reviews on social media platforms to enhance their visibility and sales. In this way, I acquire knowledge and update with the latest developments in my area of interest and support my connections on social media platforms. Since I am also a book reviewer, I get some of the book reviews published in prestigious international journals and magazines. I also endorse their books and write forewords. I receive emails seeking for my suggestions and I respond to them positively since I share my knowledge free with the world through my blogs and LinkedIn posts. This is how I add my value by investing my time and energy for my connections.

The Secrecy Behind Being the Best, Elite and Rich

"The richest people in the world look for and build networks, everyone else looks for work. Marinate on that for a minute." —Robert T. Kiyosaki

People prefer to pursue the education in prestigious institutions. Apart from acquiring knowledge from the best faculty and exchanging knowledge with their peers, they enjoy quality connections. Some of their connections reach higher positions in the long run. They help themselves since they hail from the same institution. The alumni from these institutions help their institutions to grow stronger and greater. In this way, they elevate their brand and strengthen their connections. Additionally, if you want to stay rich forever, one of the best ways is to acquire quality education in prestigious institutions as the alumni extend their help among themselves. Remember, a single contact with the right person at the right time will keep you in the right place to touch your tipping point.

Maintaining Your Network is Harder

"Effective networking isn't a result of luck – it requires hard work and persistence." —Lewis Howes

Building your network is hard and maintaining your network is harder because you must invest your time, money and energy to keep your connections growing and giving fruits to your next generation. I have come across some people from the second generation enjoying the fruits of connections from their first generation in various walks of life. Hence, don't underestimate the power of connections.

'Who You Know' versus 'What You Know'

"Who you know matters more than what you know, because when you know the right who, they will teach you the right what." —Dr. Ballanseuss

In this cutthroat competitive world what makes the successful and unsuccessful is the ability to network with others effectively. There are people who became stars due to their connections. Subsequently, they worked hard; built their skills and abilities; and retained their positions. Hence, don't underestimate the power of network and connections. In fact, ' who you know' matters more than 'what you know' in this cut-throat competitive world.

It is observed that some people are very strong in their areas but they don't know how to build connections and showcase them with others. They find it challenging and remain unnoticed and unrecognized throughout their lives. On the other hand, there are some people who have the right connections and showcase whatever the little they have and achieve recognition and success quickly. Hence ' who you know' certainly matters more than 'what you know'. If 'what you know' is the king of success, ' who you know' is the queen of success. Both king and queen are essential to run your career empire successfully. To summarize, the way hard and soft skills are essential to achieving your career success, 'what you know' and 'who you know' are equally essential to fast-track your career.

Conclusion

"It is unreasonable to think we can earn rewards without being willing to pay their true price. It is always our choice whether or not we wish to pay the price for life's rewards." —Epictetus

Social media is a powerful platform to build your connections and enhance your network. Hence, utilize it effectively by building a team of quality connections globally with a positive, right and strong attitude. Help them and seek their help. Reshuffle your team with changing times and technologies as per your principles and philosophies and based on their reciprocal response to achieve success in all spheres of your life.

"Time is the most precious element of human existence. The successful person knows how to put energy into time and how to draw success from time." —Denis Waitley

References

https://www.amazon.com/Build-Your-Dream-Network-Hyper-Connected/dp/0143111485

https://www.forbes.com/sites/nextavenue/2014/09/11/are-women-too-timid-when-they-job-search

https://www.entrepreneur.com/article/305542

18 – Leverage Social Media

"If you make customers unhappy in the physical world, they might each tell 6 friends. If you make customers unhappy on the Internet, they can each tell 6,000 friends." —Jeff Bezos

Social media has played a crucial role to highlight various social issues including women empowerment. It has highlighted many issues which were unnoticed. It has connected all people globally and brought democracy virtually. Although it has created chaos in some aspects, it has transformed society by highlighting social justice and bringing social change. Women are better informed than ever before due to the internet and advanced technology. There is growing awareness and assertiveness to fight for their equality.

You can communicate with anybody on social media across nations, time zones, and demographics. You can share your vision, mission and execution and your knowledge, skills, and abilities. It is an open platform for everyone either to agree or disagree with what you have posted. It is a democratic platform to exchange ideas, insights, opinions, and views. It is a great opportunity thrown open to humans by the technology. Therefore, women leaders must express their ambitions early in their careers to reach top positions and spread their words on social media to get noticed. To be successful on social media, you must be consistent in your content and communication. It takes lots of efforts, energy, and time to build your brand. It requires loads of passion, patience, and perseverance. In this chapter, we will discuss social media and its usage vis-à-vis women leaders.

Social Media to Build Your Career

"Most bloggers who rise above the clutter are quite often prolific–they work hard, not just writing content but networking, engaging in Social Media and more." —Darren Rowse

Technology has become both a boon and bane and it all depends on how you view it. Instead of viewing it as your enemy, you must treat it as your ally to harness it effectively to achieve human progress and prosperity. There are many people who viewed it as an ally and participated in social media to share their knowledge, ideas, insights, and opinions. There are people who leveraged social media to build their brands and fast-track their careers. Women leaders including Oprah Winfrey, Sheryl Sandberg, and Arianna Huffington have successfully leveraged social media to brand and market themselves. Of course, they have made decent money also. Hence, women must know how to leverage this amazing platform to fast-track their careers.

Tips to Fast-track Your Career on Social Media

"Build it, and they will come" only works in the movies. Social Media is a "build it, nurture it, engage them, and they may come and stay." —Seth Godin

If you are a novice, here is how you can proceed on social media. Understand the basics of all social media platforms and its pros and cons. Shortlist the ones that suit your profile, area, and image. Stick to those platforms and share your ideas, insights, thoughts, knowledge, skills, and abilities regularly. Gradually people will notice and follow you. Comment on their posts and they will reciprocate if they find the time and feel that your posts or comments are interesting. Be consistent in your posts and messages. Build your credibility. Be persistent because it takes a lot of time. At the same time don't get addicted to social media. Fix some time every day and use it judiciously without hampering your core activities and assignments. Use your filler time in the day such as traveling while you commute to your office. In this way, you can leverage your traveling time judiciously to build your brand and market yourself. Here are some tools for women leaders to adopt to excel personally, professionally, and socially. Don't shy to market and brand yourself. Be visible on social media to showcase your strengths and achievements. Make a noise whenever you achieve something worthwhile to enable the people to notice you become an inspiration for others. Here is a caution: Be careful about what you are posting. Avoid posting on sensitive issues related to religion and politics. Avoid kicking up controversies for getting short-term fame.

Conclusion

"You can never go wrong by investing in communities and the human beings within them." —Pam Moore

Social media highlighted women empowerment and atrocities on women thus advocating gender equality globally. It unfolded many things which were unknown to many people. Therefore, women must use social media judiciously to fight for their rights and fast-track their careers. To conclude, go along with the flow to leverage technology especially the social media to fast-track your career and build your leadership brand.

"Good content always has an objective; it's created with intent. It, therefore, carries triggers to action." —Ann Handley

> 39% of global respondents use social media to fill their time. From a marketing perspective, it's difficult to discern specifics activities but it's likely viewing feeds and communications. 37% of global respondents use social media to find entertaining content. Use opportunity because Sprout Social's Social Advertising Content Research reveals consistent trends. Specifically, consumers want to be entertained (41%) or taught (33%).

Reference

https://heidicohen.com/2018-social-media-use-research/

19 – Humanize Your Leadership Brand

"Your brand is what people say about you when you are not in the room" —Jeff Bezos

These are the days of branding and marketing whether you are a spiritual leader, religious leader, business leader, political leader or an academic leader. With the advent of social media, people started using technology aggressively to build their credibility and enhance visibility. There are celebrities including film stars, cricketers and sportspersons who hire marketing people and social media managers to click photographs with their pets and post on social media. They meet poor people in developing nations and the less fortunate; click photos and upload on social media platforms especially on Instagram to enhance their visibility. They want to show visually that they are committed to making a difference. Are they honestly humanizing their brands?

Humanize Your Brand

"If people believe they share values with a company, they will stay loyal to the brand." —Howard Shultz

By leveraging social media, ordinary individuals excelled as extraordinary individuals by branding and marketing aggressively. There are several celebrities who bank on the support of other celebrities to leverage their brands rather than to extend opportunities to the average individuals and upcoming ambitious individuals. Such celebrities hardly humanize their brands.

When you look at Mahatma Gandhi, Mother Teresa, Martin Luther King Jr and Nelson Mandela they worked for their causes, not applause. They walked their talk. They did not crave for publicity and visibility. It was the people who spread their ideals and ideas; and struggles and sacrifices through word of mouth and built their credibility and enhanced their visibility. However, in this internet age, most celebrities pump their money to build their brands and market themselves aggressively to create more wealth. They hardly walk their talk and make a difference in the lives of people.

Brand Humanization

"Brand is the sum total of how someone perceives a particular organization. Branding is about shaping that perception." —Ashley Friedlein

Humanizing your brand means giving a human dimension to your brand by connecting with your audience and touching their lives. It is to connect with your audience emotionally, not mechanically. It is to convert invisible elements into visible elements and intangible aspects into tangible aspects. It is to include emotions with a humane touch to your brand. It gives a competitive edge to your leadership brand.

When everyone involved on social media is human why cannot you humanize your brand? To humanize your brand, you must emphasize emotions, egos, and feelings. Therefore, brand humanization can be defined as the process of giving a human dimension to your brand by involving emotions, egos, and feelings to connect with your audience quickly to touch their lives and make a difference. In this age of automation, it is essential to emphasize human elements to your brand due to the dearth of physical proximity. Humanizing your brand is a marathon, not a sprint. It requires regular efforts, energy, enthusiasm and time to humanize your brand.

Tips to Humanize Your Brand

"Your personal brand is a promise to your clients...a promise of quality, consistency, competency, and reliability" —Jason Hartman, Author of *Become The Brand Of Choice*

Stephen J. Sampson in his book, *Leaders without Titles* unfolds that horizontal leaders have six human attributes that attract others to them, even though they have no authority over others. They are physicality, intellectuality, sociability, emotionality, personability, and morality. Hence, emphasize these attributes to humanize your brand. Additionally, if you can humanize your brand with egos, emotions, and feelings you will be successful as an individual leader and organizational leader. Here are some tips to humanize your brand.

- Emphasize social issues to bring social change.
- Take up a few core issues globally and highlight them.
- Focus on average individuals and their issues to explore ideas.
- Include emotional elements to touch the hearts and offer inspiring ideas to ignite their minds.
- Accept your mistakes and apologize. Don't worry about flaws. Accept flaws and failures because nobody is perfect in the world.
- Keep people before profit.
- Avoid short-term temptations.

Be agile and active. Engage your audience on your social media platform. Encourage agreement and disagreement. Be honest and transparent. Observe ethics and etiquette. Build trust and goodwill in the audience. Build social media warriors and soldiers. Build brand ambassadors and evangelists. Walk your talk and go an extra mile. Above all, learn, unlearn and relearn to humanize your leadership brand constantly.

There are people who kick up controversies to get noticed on social media. They want instant fame on social media. Such tactics don't help them in the long run because consistent growth in the graph is essential to building your brand on social media. However, there will be occasional setbacks in career graphs. When you look at the authentic influencers they mean business and grow consistently on social media with meaningful dialogues and discussions by sharing great content consistently and adding value to their audiences.

If you think that brands are like humans on the move, you will personalize, engage and inspire your audiences effectively and successfully. When you look at global companies including Google, Apple, Facebook, Nike, Coca-Cola, South West Airlines, McDonald, and Starbucks, they humanized their brands successfully. They emphasized customer delight which is far ahead of customer satisfaction. When you humanize your brand you can achieve customer delight.

Conclusion

"Your brand is the single most important investment you can make in your business." —Steve Forbes

People have become much wiser and smarter than ever before because social media has thrown everything open to assess individuals and their activities. It reviews and offers feedback instantly. The audiences watch their leaders from all spheres; branding and marketing tactics; and assess authenticity. Hence, ordinary individuals who aspire to excel as extraordinary individuals and successful individuals who intend to become more influential must add value to others by humanizing their brands and making a difference to the world.

"Products are made in a factory but brands are created in the mind." —Walter Landor

> If you achieve success overnight you miss valuable lessons along the way.

Reference

https://www.brandingstrategyinsider.com/2017/02/building-six-attributes-human-centric-brands.html#.W6mZF2gzbIU

20 – Build Women CEOs Globally

"Women share this planet 50/50 and they are underrepresented—their potential astonishingly untapped."
—Emma Watson

Encouraging women and emphasizing diversity help improve organizational bottom lines. However, very few organizations follow these principles globally. Although everyone talks about women empowerment and participation in the corporate world aggressively, very few organizations follow them in spirit. In fact, women encounter more challenges than men from recruitment to retirement and from entry to exit in global organizations.

Lay the Ladder for Women CEOs Globally

"Go through some difficult experiences. If you can live through them and learn from them, you have a much better chance of knowing what to do when the chips are down and everyone else is freaking out." —Debra A. Cafaro

The CEO of the company must be an all-rounder. She must be a jack of all trades and expert in her area. She must know the length and breadth of everything and depth of the core domain. It is usually possible for executives who are from the technical domain. The CEO must be a troubleshooter, crisis manager, communicator, strategist, and a visionary. The CEO must change as per the situation and act decisively. She must apply different strokes to different people in different situations which may not be possible for ordinary leaders. She must be flexible with the stakeholders to get the tasks executed successfully.

Although women are more emotional than men, they know how to make decisions in a stressful environment. To be successful CEOs, women must have high energy, grit, ego-strength, and the ability to bounce back from failures with tenacity and resilience. Here are some more qualities that are essential to step into the shoes of CEOs—strategic vision, continuous learning, adaptability, engaging employees, managing VUCA (volatility, uncertainty, complexity, and ambiguity), building connections and balancing stakeholders to name a few. Succinctly, to become a CEO, the woman leader must acquire technical and business acumen; hard and soft skills; and apply hard and soft power as per the situation.

Strategies for Global Organizations to Build Women CEOs

Here are some strategies for global organizations to build women chief executives.

- Identify the potential women in the early stage to keep them in the leadership pipeline. Lay the ladder for their leadership development.
- Create a conducive environment to enable them to fast-track their career.
- Encourage them to pursue line positions, not staff positions. Inform them to acquire emotional intelligence.
- Emphasize building credibility because building credibility is the first step toward effective leadership.
- Encourage them to build their personal and professional brands to stand out from others.
- Encourage girl scouts.
- Remove the prevailing strong perception that men are promoted due to potential while women are promoted due to performance.

- Adopt an integrated approach and ensure coordinated efforts from all stakeholders including organizations, women associations, nonprofits, and government to build women CEOs globally.

It is a well-admitted fact that the organizations with high proportions of senior women leaders deliver stronger financial results. Hence, global organizations including IBM, Apple, Facebook, Accenture, Deloitte, Chevron, Coca-Cola and Bank of America emphasized the importance of women leaders and some of them committed to grooming women leaders as CEOs. Accenture has set bold goals to ensure 25 percent of women managing directors by 2020 and achieve a gender-balanced workforce by 2025. These are all the steps in the right direction. More global companies must come forward to empower women to excel as CEOs to build a better corporate world.

> Companies with women holding at least 30% of leadership roles are 1.4 times more likely to have sustained, profitable growth, and are 1.7 times more likely to have greater leadership strength.

Routes to Corner Office

"The thing women have yet to learn is nobody gives you power. You just take it." —Roseanne Barr

Women need coaches and mentors to shape their careers. The onus lies with organizations to engage passionate coaches and mentors to groom them as CEOs. Additionally, women must be ready to shoulder challenging roles and responsibilities. They must demonstrate courage and conviction. They must avoid the fear of failure and criticism. They must earn their titles by working hard and smart. They must not expect any sympathy from men because of their gender. They must come forward to encounter challenges on par with men to excel. It is improper to accuse men of their present plight. They must fight for their equal rights to assert themselves.

It is a well-admitted fact that men oversell, and women undersell. Hence, women should not hesitate to sell themselves. They must showcase their competencies and capabilities regularly. They must shed their traditional mindset and wed unconventional mindset to market themselves both within and outside the workplace to get noticed for their contributions and achievements.

Smash through the Glass Ceiling!

"Leadership is hard to define and good leadership even harder. But if you can get people to follow you to the ends of the earth, you are a great leader." —Indra Nooyi

Seize the opportunities to smash through the glass ceiling to excel as a CEO. Don't conceal your potential under the mountain with phobias and apprehensions. Keep honor before money to stand out as a role model for others. Remember that the race to top leadership slot is not an easy thing. It is very challenging to scale to top slot and stay there.

Create a Gender Equal World

"A wise woman wishes to be no one's enemy; a wise woman refuses to be anyone's victim." —Maya Angelou

The world is at the crossroad currently. It is time for men to advocate gender equality globally. Remember that it is not a women's issue anymore but a human rights issue. Hence, make your voice heard to achieve a gender equal world. Building women movements globally to ensure women empowerment helps to some extent. However, women supporting themselves helps greatly to ensure gender equality globally. Additionally, men must extend their hands to women wholeheartedly to build an honorable and prosperous world.

When a woman reaches a top slot, she is more capable than men. There is a need for all of us to break the stereotypes. Women should break their traditional mental and psychological barriers and shoulder leadership roles and responsibilities. They must work harder to prove themselves to excel as leaders in this male-dominated society. Remember that the society cannot grow when one sex is denied with opportunities. It is essential to allow both sexes to excel equally based on merit and talent. It requires empathy on the part of men and a big heart to handhold women to groom them as global leaders. If women also participate in leadership roles and responsibilities, we will find a better society with lots of prosperity and stability.

Conclusion

"There is no royal flower-strewn path to success. And if there is, I have not found it, for if I have accomplished anything in life it is because I have been willing to work hard." —Madam C.J. Walker

Both men and women are biologically different. That difference cannot be treated as a deficiency. It is natural for them to lead differently. Let us understand and appreciate the differences and respect them. Let us look at women not from the gender perspective but from the human perspective and judge their competencies and qualifications purely based on merit. Let us look at women with new lenses. Handhold women and take them forward to leadership positions to enable them to endeavor and explore to achieve leadership effectiveness and success. To summarize, women are equal to men in all spheres. They are proving their mettle globally to assert themselves. However, they must work harder to prove themselves. They must accept the fact that there is no free lunch in the world. They must express their ambition in the early stage of their careers and work hard consistently and relentlessly with a focus and vision to excel as CEOs globally.

"You're not in competition with other women. You're in competition with everyone." —Tina Fey

Reference

https://www.ddiworld.com/glf2018/diversity-leaders

21 – WHEN WOMEN RISE,
WE ALL RISE

"If you educate a man you educate an individual, but if you educate a woman you educate a nation." —African Proverb

A great world is possible only when men are educated about the empowerment of women. A great world is possible only when women dare to dream and achieve big. A great world is possible only when men and women collaborate to unlock their potential. In this concluding chapter, we will discuss education and empowerment to unlock the potential of the human race to build a peaceful and prosperous world.

We must enlighten men about the importance of women empowerment and educate women to make them confident, competent and independent. According to UNICEF, "When we educate a girl, we not only give her the tools and knowledge to make her own decisions and shape her own future, we also help raise the standard of living of her family and her community." Encouraging girl's education helps in many ways to empower women. It reduces child marriage and infant mortality. It controls the population explosion and decreases domestic violence. It helps them understand the world, acquire the knowledge, skills, and abilities to grab the employment opportunities and excel economically. It helps them assert themselves in the political process. It helps them make the right decisions and lead an independent life without any pulls and pressures. Above all, it helps build a prosperous and peaceful world. Greg Mortenson remarked, "You can hand out condoms, drop bombs, build roads, or put in electricity, but until the girls are educated a society won't change."

Collaboration is Key

"Women will have achieved true equality when men share with them the responsibility of bringing up the next generation." — Ruth Bader Ginsburg

Men must change their mindset the way they look at women. They must empathize with women and the women must break their mental barriers. Men must handhold women and women must dream big to make it big. Women should not shy away from shouldering their responsibilities. They must break their mental barriers and move forward aggressively. Here are some ideas and insights for men and women to collaborate to create a gender-equal world.

- Men must empathize with women and understand their expectations, offer opportunities and support women to be leaders and inspire them to accomplish their dreams and objectives.
- Women must unite in their dedication to empower one another, to create opportunities, and to lift up their communities as they lift up themselves.
- Women must not expect men to create lives for them. Instead, they must create their own lives. It provides a sense of satisfaction and happiness for women that they have created their own lives.
- Women must have power over themselves, not on men. They must treat men as allies, not enemies to achieve gender equality globally.

Steps to Achieve Gender Equality Globally

"Women will be hidden no more. We will not remain hidden figures. We have names... It was the woman that gave you Dr. Martin Luther King, Jr. It was the woman that gave you Malcolm X. And according to the Bible, it was a woman that gave you Jesus. Don't you ever forget it." —Janelle Monáe

It is unfortunate that women are abused physically, mentally, and emotionally in some countries across the world. Men and women must understand that they cannot live without each other. Hence, there must be empathy and mutual respect to each other.

Educated men will treat women like queens. Hence, provide education to men. Men must change their attitude toward women. They must respect the choices of women. Women must assert their rights. They must dream big and convert their weaknesses into strengths. They must believe in themselves. They must do what they love. They must follow their passion.

Parents must educate their male children to treat women with dignity and respect. They must not clip the wings of their children. They must encourage their children to dream and achieve big in their lives.

Offer equal access to education for women. Invest in policies and programs. Coordinated efforts from all stakeholders including educators, students, parents, government, thought leaders, intellectuals, and nonprofits are essential to achieving gender equality globally.

Lead from the Front

"Feminism isn't about making women strong. Women are already strong. It's about changing the way the world perceives that strength." —G.D. Anderson

Globally the encouragement to women empowerment is amazing except in a few Asian countries due to cultural factors and religious practices. Hence, women must avail the present opportunities to excel in all sectors to leave their marks.

We cannot force men to sacrifice their careers for women. Instead, we can implore men to support women in whatever the best possible way to achieve women empowerment and advancement. Women must chart their own paths to prove themselves identifying their inner talents and understanding their limitations.

When Women Rise, We all Rise

Women empowerment is not only a gender issue but also diversity, social and economic issue globally.

"Human rights are women's rights and women's rights are human rights, once and for all." —Hillary Clinton

Gender equality is no more a male or female issue. It is more of a human issue to achieve overall development of both genders. Therefore, treat gender equality as a fundamental human right.

Empowering women is essential to achieve human progress and gender equality globally. When you want to achieve growth and prosperity it is imperative to encourage women participation in the developmental activities. A bird cannot fly with one wing because it needs two wings to fly. Similarly, when you want the society to progress, you must advocate women empowerment and encourage the participation of women who constitute half of the global population. When both men and women participate, imagine the type of society we will pass on to our next generation. Hence, men must support women wholeheartedly to allow the latter to unlock their potential and contribute to the global society. Remember, when women rise, we all rise.

Women empowerment must not be misunderstood as an initiative against men, but it is to ensure equal opportunities for women to excel in their lives. Hence, view it positively to bring a positive change in global society. To conclude, both men and women must come forward to advocate gender equality globally to build a peaceful, prosperous and honorable world.

"The day will come when men will recognize woman as his peer, not only at the fireside, but in councils of the nation. Then, and not until then, will there be the perfect comradeship, the ideal union between the sexes that shall result in the highest development of the race." —Susan B. Anthony

References

Author's Vision 2030: https://professormsraovision2030.blogspot.com

Author's Amazon URL: http://www.amazon.com/M.-S.-Rao/e/B00MB63BKM

Author's LinkedIn: https://in.linkedin.com/in/professormsrao

Author's You Tube: http://www.youtube.com/user/profmsr7

Author's Google Plus: https://plus.google.com/+ProfessorMSRao

Author's Facebook page: https://www.facebook.com/Professor-MS-Rao-451516514937414/

Author's Company Facebook Page: https://www.facebook.com/MSR-Leadership-Consultants-India-375224215917499/

Author's Instagram: https://www.instagram.com/professormsrao

Author's Blogs:

http://professormsraoguru.blogspot.com

http://professormsrao.blogspot.com

http://profmsr.blogspot.com

https://www.buildon.org/wp-content/uploads/2016/02/IWD-2016-Book_final2.pdf

"One life is all we have and we live it as we believe in living it. But to sacrifice what you are and to live without belief, that is a fate more terrible than dying." —Joan of Arc

Appendix A
Soft Leadership and Women Leadership

"Our emerging workforce is not interested in command and control leadership. They don't want to do things because I said so, they want to do things because they want to do them." —Irene Rosenfield

Soft leadership is a new leadership perspective that is closely connected with women leadership. Hence, we will discuss soft leadership and its relevance to women leadership.

Women leadership can be defined as the process of women leading from the front with an example by managing the emotions, egos, and feelings of all people especially men by breaking the glass ceiling to accomplish organizational goals and objectives.

What is Soft Leadership?
"First they ignore you, then they laugh at you, then they fight you, then you win." — Mahatma Gandhi

I joined my Ph.D. in the area of soft skills in 2007. I wanted to provide sanctity to the discipline of soft skills. So, I worked hard and created several triggers and finally earned my Ph.D. in 2011. Since I joined the Indian Air Force when I was 19 years, I developed a keen interest in leadership. I clubbed soft skills with leadership and coined soft leadership. During my training programs, the executives expressed their unhappiness over the prevailing leadership styles. Hence, I decided to coin a new leadership style—soft leadership. There are 11 Cs that constitute soft leadership—character, charisma, conscience, conviction, courage, communication, compassion, commitment, consistency, consideration and contribution. Here are the inspiring examples connected with each C. Mahatma Gandhi is associated with character, Mikhail Gorbachev with charisma, Martin Luther King Jr with conscience, Aung San Sui Kyi with convictions, Alexander the Great with courage, Winston Churchill with communication, Mother Teresa with compassion, Nelson Mandela with commitment, John Wesley with consistency, Dalai Lama with consideration and Booker T. Washington with contribution. It is highly challenging for people to cultivate these 11 characteristics. However, if people possess more than 6 traits they get into the fold of soft leadership.

I requested Dave Ulrich, father of modern HR who is my good friend to create leadership code and he consented and mapped 11 Cs onto leadership code thus giving sanctity to soft leadership. I published several books and research papers on soft leadership. International Leadership Association invited me to participate in a webinar on this leadership. I participated and shared my ideas and insights on soft leadership.

Soft leadership is people-oriented leadership without compromising the task-orientation. It is to accomplish goals and objectives through persuasion, not through pressure. It is to lead with soft skills and people skills. It blends soft skills, hard skills, and leadership. It emphasizes the significance of precious Human Resources. It helps in managing the emotions, egos, and feelings of the people successfully. It focuses on the personality, attitude, and behavior of the people, and calls for making others feel important. It is an integrative, participative, relationship, and behavioral leadership model adopting tools such as persuasion, negotiation, recognition, appreciation, motivation, and collaboration to accomplish the tasks effectively. Succinctly, soft leadership can be defined as the process of setting goals; influencing people through persuasion; building strong teams; negotiating them with a win-win attitude; respecting their failures; handholding them; motivating them constantly; aligning their energies and efforts; recognizing and appreciating their contribution in accomplishing organizational goals and objectives with an emphasis on soft skills. It is based on the right mindset, skill set, and toolset. Here is the diagram (Figure 1) connecting 11 C's that collectively constitute soft leadership.

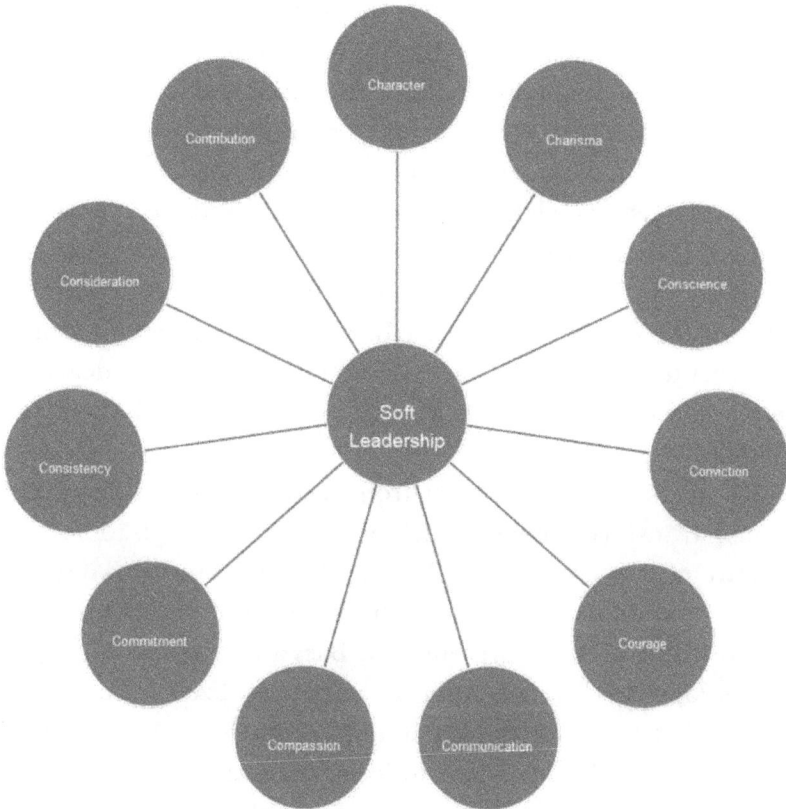

Figure 1 The Eleven Cs of Soft Leadership

Since the world is changing fast, this leadership perspective is very much essential. With the entry of millennials who are smart and ambitious, this leadership perspective is more essential than ever before. Additionally, this leadership style is the need of the hour with the advent of Artificial Intelligence and Fourth Industrial Revolution.

Soft Leadership and Other Leadership Styles

"No one cares how much you know until they know how much you care." —Theodore Roosevelt

Soft leadership is different from other leadership styles especially servant leadership and transformational leadership. Robert Greenleaf coined servant leadership which contains 10 characteristics—listening, empathy, healing, awareness, persuasion, conceptualization, foresight, stewardship, commitment to the growth of people, and building community; while soft leadership contains 11 characteristics—character, charisma, conscience, conviction, courage, communication, compassion, commitment, consistency, consideration, and contribution. Hence, both are different. The main objective of servant leadership is to have a servant attitude and heart to serve the people. However, soft leadership deals with the manner in which leaders lead others to accomplish their goals and objectives.

Soft leadership is different from transformational leadership because transformational leadership emphasizes 4 Is. The main objective of transformational leadership is to transform individuals and institutions. Soft leadership comprises of 11 Cs while transformational leadership presented by Bass and Avolio comprises of four I's (a) inspirational motivation, (b) idealized influence, (c) individualized consideration, and (d) intellectual stimulation. Transformational leaders lead followers to levels of higher morals. Soft leadership involves handling the people with soft skills and people skills to get the tasks executed effectively while transformational leadership involves in transforming the individuals and institutions with the help of 4Is. Additionally, according to Burns, the transformational leadership explains that both the leader and the follower lift each other to higher levels of morality and motivation.

Dave Ulrich's Interpretation Of 11Cs

Dave Ulrich, the Partner of The RBL Group has interpreted 11Cs by mapping onto leadership code as follows:

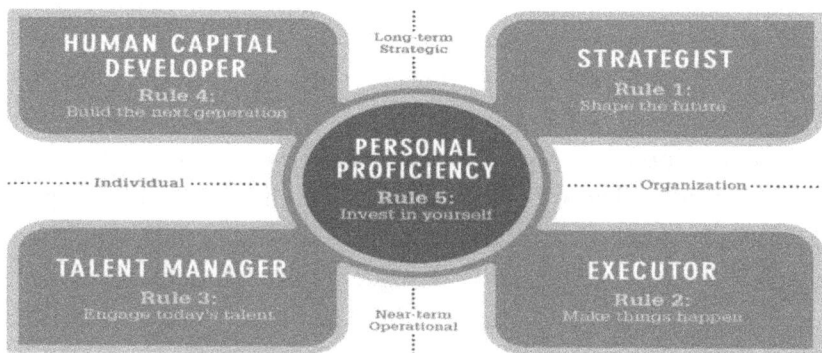

Dave Ulrich's Leadership Code (Figure 2)

Strategists: Strategists answer the question "where are we going?" and make sure that those around them understand the direction as well. They not only envision but also can create a future. They figure out where the organization needs to go to succeed, they test these ideas pragmatically against current resources (money, people, organizational capabilities), and they work with others to figure out how to get from the present to the desired future. Strategists have a point of view about the future and are able to position their organization to create and respond to that future.

Executors: The Executor dimension of the leadership code focuses on the question "How will we make sure we get to where we are going?" Executors translate strategy into action, make change happy, assign accountability, know which key decisions to take and which to delegate, and make sure that teams work well together. They keep promises to multiple stakeholders. The rules for executors revolve around disciplines for getting things done and the technical expertise to get the right things done right.

Talent Managers: Leaders who optimize talent today answer the question "Who goes with us on our business journey?" Talent managers know how to identify, build and engage talent to get results now. Talent managers identify what skills are required, draw talent to their organizations, engage them, communicate extensively, and ensure that employees turn in their best efforts. Talent managers generate intense personal, professional and organizational loyalty. The rules for talent managers center around resolutions that help people develop themselves for the good of the organization.

Human Capital Developers: Leaders who are Human Capital Developers answer the question, "who stays and sustains the organization for the next generation?" Talent Managers ensure shorter-term results through people while Human Capital Developers ensure that the organization has the longer-term competencies required for future strategic success. Just as good parents invest in helping their children succeed, human capital developers help future leaders be successful. Human Capital Developers throughout the organization build a workforce plan focused on future talent, understand how to develop future talent, and help employees see their future careers within the company. Human Capital Developers ensure that the organization will outlive any single individual. Human Capital Developers install rules that demonstrate a pledge to building the next generation of talent.

But, what was found at the heart of great leadership was what we called *personal proficiency*. Effective leaders cannot be reduced to what they know and do. Who they are as human beings has everything to do with how much they can accomplish with and through other people. Leaders are learners: from success, failure, assignments, books, classes, people, and life itself. Passionate about their beliefs and interests, they expend enormous personal energy and attention on whatever matters to them. Effective leaders inspire loyalty and goodwill in others because they themselves act with integrity and trust. Decisive and impassioned, they are capable of bold and courageous moves. Confident in their ability to deal with situations as they arise, they can tolerate ambiguity.

According to Dave Ulrich, all the 11Cs map onto the personal proficiency dimension. He further adds, "By summarizing psychological literature around personality, attitude, perceptions, and emotional intelligence, Professor M.S.Rao lays out the conceptual underpinnings of leaders who demonstrate personal proficiency, or soft leadership."

Soft Leadership versus Hard Leadership

Hard leadership emphasizes more on tasks and less on people while the soft leadership emphasizes more on people to get the tasks executed. Political leaders including George Washington, Franklin Roosevelt, Mahatma Gandhi, Martin Luther King Jr., Mikhail Gorbachev, Angela Merkel, and Aung San Sui Kyi fall in the category of soft leadership while Harry Truman, Joseph McCarthy, Charles de Gaulle, Lee Kwan Yew, and Margaret Thatcher fall in the category of hard leadership. Corporate leaders like Jeff Immelt former CEO of General Electric and Timothy Cook of Apple Computers fall in the bracket of soft leadership while Jack Welch and Steve Jobs fall in the category of hard leadership.

Soft Leadership and Women Leadership

"The strongest natures, when they are influenced, submit the most unreservedly; it is perhaps a sign of their strength." —Virginia Woolf

To excel as successful soft leaders, it is ideal to acquire 11Cs— character, charisma, conscience, conviction, courage, communication, compassion, commitment, consistency, consideration and contribution. However, to excel as successful women leaders, it is essential to acquire six characteristics—character, conscience, courage, compassion, commitment, and contribution.

> Women rate higher in overall leadership effectiveness than their male counterparts, with the greatest gap evident at the highest executive levels.

Women Leadership—Six Characteristics

"You have to look at leadership through the eyes of the followers and you have to live the message. What I have learned is that people become motivated when you guide them to the source of their own power and when you make heroes out of employees who personify what you want to see in the organization." —Anita Roddick

Character: Warren Bennis says, "Successful leadership is not about being tough or soft, sensitive or assertive, but about a set of attributes. First and foremost is the character." The collapse of companies like Enron, Lehman Brothers, and World Com reminds the world about the leaders lacking character at their core. People sometimes blame the business schools for producing such leaders without any ethical and moral values. However, we cannot blame business schools for all the ills that happened at the business houses globally. The problem lies with the leaders who lack strong character resulting in such downfalls.

The character is one of the key components of soft leaders. It is through their strong character they lead their people by influencing and guiding them. People look at leaders who have impeccable integrity and who walk the talk. Hence, most companies emphasize character during leadership development programs. For instance, companies like Hindustan Lever emphasizes character wherein an individual puts his company's needs before his own. It has a strong human resource management system and emphasizes a strong ethical system and character among its employees.

As a leader, you are always under the scanner. You need to set the right example through an impeccable character in order to grow as a leader. People have the tendency to look at the weaknesses rather than the strengths of others. Hence, it is essential to demonstrate strong character to lead from the front to influence people around you.

Martin Luther King, Jr. said, "The ultimate measure of a man is not where he stands in moments of comfort and convenience, but where he stands at times of challenge and controversy." The character is the key thing that differentiates between good leaders from others. In fact, a good character makes a person a great leader. What counts at the end of the day or your life is who you are, not what you have.

Conscience: Sophocles said, "There is no witness so terrible and no accuser so powerful as conscience which dwells within us." Conscience is one of the major key components of soft leaders as clear conscience makes them stand out from other leaders. People expect leaders to be ethical and responsible. They also look up to leaders whose conscience cares for them. Conscience differentiates right from the wrong. Leaders must have clear conscience to convince themselves to enable them to persuade others. If there is a chasm between the word and the deed conscience reminds the same. Mahatma Gandhi was always clear with his conscience. He unveiled the mistakes he had made in his life in his autobiography. Every person makes mistakes but how many unveil and admit the same. In fact, it requires a lot of courage to reveal wrong-doings on their part.

Several leaders resigned because of their conscience. They left their high positions due to the call from their conscience. Hence, conscience is powerful. Leaders must convince their conscience first to convince others. Aung San Suu Kyi underwent several trials and tribulations from military rulers during the house arrest as her conscience did not allow her to leave the country. Mahatma Gandhi led the Civil Disobedience movement which was a non-violent protest against the British. It was an act of conscience.

Dr. Martin Luther King aptly said, "Justice is a temporary thing that must, at last, come to an end; but the conscience is eternal and will never die." Several problems and evils in the society are the results of people compromising with their conscience. People may cheat others, not their conscience. Conscience is always clear, and it is powerful. People must be accountable to their conscience. People may do several wrong things for their survival or their selfish motives. Ultimately they need to persuade their conscience which is always clear. It is a reminder for every human being. Hence, don't compromise with your conscience as compromising with a conscience is equal to the death of a person morally.

Courage: Courage is an integral part of soft leadership. According to Aristotle, courage is the first virtue, because it makes all of the other virtues possible. Courage does not mean fighting physically with others. Courage doesn't mean killing people ruthlessly. Courage doesn't mean being aggressive all times. Mark Twain rightly remarked, "Courage is resistance to fear, mastery of fear – not absence of fear." Courage is about standing by your values and morals and principles and policies despite being pressurized by others and receiving threats from others. People often believe that courage as a characteristic is confined to military personnel alone. That is not true. Courage is essential for everyone. Courage is also a major key component for soft leaders because courage commands confidence from their followers.

People always want leaders with backbone. David versus Goliath is an amazing example where tiny David took on the mighty Goliath successfully. A few leaders proved globally that it is not the size but the strength counts. When we take the example of the Yugoslavian leader, Marshal Tito he broke the back of the Soviet empire. President Ronald Reagan, Pope John Paul II, and Prime Minister Margaret Thatcher came together to bring down the crumbling walls of the Soviet Union, giving hundreds of millions of people the chance to enjoy freedom. The leader like Lee Kuan Yew brought Singapore from nowhere to a prosperous country despite scarcity in natural resources. All these leaders made a difference in this world through their courageous leadership. What counts at the end of life is neither the muscle power nor the money power but your willpower.

Compassion: When we look at soft leaders like Lord Jesus and Buddha, we find them being filled with compassion. They changed the face of the world with their compassion. The soft leader like Mother Teresa helped lepers and poor through her selfless service. She made an immense difference in the lives of poor and downtrodden in India. In fact, compassion is an integral characteristic of soft leadership. It helps to connect with others easily. People appreciate the leaders who care for them.

Compassion means caring for others by ignoring your own interests. Compassion is not weakness. Kahlil Gibran says, "Tenderness and kindness are not signs of weakness and despair but manifestations of strength and resolution." Compassion is all about genuinely caring for your people. It is handholding them without expecting any returns. Compassion commands great inner strength, courage, and power. Compassion is a key to ministering to people. Compassion makes a huge difference in making leaders as soft leaders. Soft leadership flows from the fountain of compassion.

The real leaders are the ones who encourage others, care for others, empathize and demonstrate compassion with others. Only such leaders have the ability to influence and maximize the potential of their people and organizations.

Commitment: Soft leaders have another great characteristic of commitment as it makes them command respect among others. It is their firm commitment toward their causes that wins acclaim from others. If you want your life to be successful you must be committed. For instance, when you love your family, you must demonstrate your firm commitment. Commitment consumes your time. But it builds longevity in relations. As a leader, if you demonstrate your commitment people trust you and treat you with the utmost respect. It is rightly said, people don't care how big you are. They only care how committed you are. We find several families breaking due to lack of commitment. We also find teams getting crashed at the workplace due to the dearth of commitment. Commitment is the bridge between the word and the deed. A firm commitment toward your word and work makes you as a successful leader.

Contribution: Stephan Girard said, "If I thought I was going to die tomorrow, I should nevertheless plant a tree today." We are what we are here today because of amazing contributions made by several soft leaders to this mankind regardless of their areas of interest. The contribution includes precious time, money, energy, ideas, knowledge, and assistance to society. Genuine and selfless contribution takes to true leadership. People respect the leaders who contribute their best to society without hankering for wealth, power or prestige.

Mother Teresa once remarked, "We ourselves feel that what we are doing is just a drop in the ocean. But the ocean would be less because of that missing drop." While contributing to others it can be in small portions. People often think that the contribution must be in a big way. In fact, a small effort is better than no effort. A huge amount of small contributions makes up to a large amount of differences for society. It is rightly said, "All the whining and complaining in the world is not going to make a difference to the world. It will only drain you of your precious energy from doing things that do make a difference." Hence, contribute your best little by little consistently, and you would be amazed at the differences that you make to the society over a period of time.

To conclude, acquire six characteristics—character, conscience, courage, compassion, commitment and contribution to excel as a successful woman leader and CEO.

"Just because you are CEO, don't think you have landed. You must continually increase your learning, the way you think, and the way you approach the organization. I've never forgotten that."
—Indra Nooyi

References
http://www.amazon.com/Soft-Leadership-Make-others-important/dp/8175156538

https://www.amazon.com/21-Success-Sutras-Ceos-Rao/dp/162865290X

https://www.amazon.com/Soft-Skills-Overcome-Workplace-Challenges/dp/1628653035

http://www.emeraldinsight.com/journals.htm?articleid=17087126

http://onlinelibrary.wiley.com/doi/10.1002/ltl.20019/abstract

http://www.ila-net.org/Webinars/Archive/Rao082012.html

REFERENCES

Author's Vision 2030: https://professormsraovision2030.blogspot.com

Author's Amazon URL: http://www.amazon.com/M.-S.-Rao/e/ B00MB63BKM

Author's LinkedIn: https://in.linkedin.com/in/professormsrao

Author's You Tube: http://www.youtube.com/user/profmsr7

Author's Google Plus: https://plus.google.com/+ProfessorMSRao

Author's Facebook page: https://www.facebook.com/Professor-MS-Rao-451516514937414/

Author's Company Facebook Page: https://www.facebook.com/ MSR-Leadership-Consultants-India-375224215917499/

Author's Instagram: https://www.instagram.com/professormsrao

Author's Blogs:

http://professormsraoguru.blogspot.com

http://professormsrao.blogspot.com

http://profmsr.blogspot.com

https://www.amazon.com/21-Success-Sutras-Ceos-Rao/dp/ 162865290X

https://www.amazon.com/Soft-Skills-Overcome-Workplace-Challenges/dp/1628653035

http://www.amazon.com/Soft-Leadership-Make-others-important/dp/8175156538

https://www.uvu.edu/uwlp/global/groups.html

https://trendwatching.com/trends/pdf/2012-03%20FLAWSOME.pdf

https://cew.org.au/wp-content/uploads/2017/09/CEW-Executive-Census-2017.pdf

https://www.webershandwick.com/uploads/news/files/female-ceo-reputation-premium-executive-summary.pdf

https://www.businessinsider.in/14-surprising-psychological-reasons-someone-might-fall-in-love-with-you/14-surprising-psychological-reasons-someone-might-fall-in-love-with-you/slideshow/57086650.cms

https://static1.squarespace.com/static/54bf1264e4b042c4bf4d7d5f/t/5ae6cdff88251bd2b3fde160/1525075775881/Do+women+really+need+help+to+progress+-+Anneli+Blundell+whitepaper.pdf

http://www.ushistory.org/us/54b.asp

https://www.nobelprize.org/prizes/peace/2014/yousafzai/auto-biography/

https://www.theguardian.com/world/2015/mar/06/gender-equality-still-decades-away-un-women

www.grantthornton.cn/upload/IBR_2013_Women_in_senior_management_EN.pdf

https://engage.kornferry.com/womenceosspeak

https://hbr.org/2016/04/do-women-make-bolder-leaders-than-men

https://www.ddiworld.com/DDI/media/trend-research/holding-women-back_tr_ddi.pdf?ext=.pdf

https://images.dowjones.com/wp-content/uploads/sites/137/2017/07/31153316/WITW_2015_JournalReport.pdf

https://www.deakinco.com/uploads/news/Anneli_Blundell_white-paper.pdf

https://www.ncbi.nlm.nih.gov/pmc/articles/PMC4641904/

http://www.cpahq.org/cpahq/cpadocs/Genderdiffe.pdf

https://www.murrayedwards.cam.ac.uk/sites/default/files/Collaborating%20with%20Men%20-%20FINAL%20Report.pdf

https://www.coastal.edu/media/administration/.../pdf/Cinardo_Communication.pdf

http://www.uky.edu/ofa/sites/www.uky.edu.ofa/files/uploads/Gender%20Styles%20in%20Communication.pdf

https://pdfs.semanticscholar.org/4698/d2a6dfa8bd81975d8a20707c7157f95c6e97.pdf

https://www.asianmoneyguide.com/life-lessons-pepsico

https://www.vox.com/policy-and-politics/2018/6/8/17413254/
women-fortune-500-ceos-politics-blue-wave

www.rbc.com/newsroom/_assets …/pdf/Developing-Advancing-
Female-Leaders.pdf

https://limitless.insead.edu/7-deadly-myths/

http://www.heforshe.org/en/newsroom/news/champions-
announcement-2017

https://www.amazon.com/Leadership-CPR-Resuscitating-
Workplace-Performance-ebook/dp/B07CY4CSRH

https://ppw.kuleuven.be/cscp/documents/artikels-colette/the-
queen-bee-phenomenon.pdf

https://www.bustle.com/p/what-is-queen-bee-syndrome-it-
might-explain-why-some-women-are-uncivil-to-each-other-at-
work-8402852

https://www.amazon.com/Soft-Skills-Overcome-Workplace-
Challenges/dp/1628653035

https://www.emeraldinsight.com/doi/full/10.1108/OTH-06-
2017-0034

https://www.allthingsic.com/wp-content/uploads/2015/01/The-
Value-of-Soft-Skills-to-the-UK-Economy.pdf

https://www.adeccogroup.com/wp-content/themes/ado-group/
downloads/the-adecco-group-white-paper-the-soft-skills-
imperative.pdf

https://www.mckinsey.com/featured-insights/gender-equality/
women-in-the-workplace-2017

https://www.huffingtonpost.com/marilyn-nagel/women-network-
differently_b_8259538.html

https://www.entrepreneur.com/article/305542

https://heidicohen.com/2018-social-media-use-research/

https://www.theguardian.com/society/2017/nov/01/
gender-pay-gap-217-years-to-close-world-economic-forum

https://www.forbes.com/sites/shelleyzalis/2018/10/30/lessons-
from-the-worlds-most-gender-equal-countries/#376cab727dd8

https://www.forbes.com/sites/selenarezvani1/2018/04/13/
six-companies-hacking-the-gender-wage-gap/#5dc8075f7055

https://www.usatoday.com/story/life/tv/2018/10/25/highest-paid-tv-actress-sofia-vergara-tops-list/1765520002/

https://www.thepeoplespace.com/ideas/articles/how-metoo-helps-prevent-sexual-harassment-workplace

https://www.shrm.org/resourcesandtools/tools-and-samples/policies/pages/cms_000554.aspx

https://www.amazon.com/Build-Your-Dream-Network-Hyper-Connected/dp/0143111485

https://www.forbes.com/sites/nextavenue/2014/09/11/are-women-too-timid-when-they-job-search

https://www.brandingstrategyinsider.com/2017/02/building-six-attributes-human-centric-brands.html#.W6mZF2gzbIU

https://www.ddiworld.com/glf2018/diversity-leaders

https://www.inc.com/john-rampton/8-historical-power-women-leaders-stories.html

https://successstory.com/people/virginia-marie-rometty

http://fortune.com/2016/02/29/women-entrepreneurs-success/

http://www.emeraldinsight.com/journals.htm?articleid=17087126

http://onlinelibrary.wiley.com/doi/10.1002/ltl.20019/abstract

http://www.ila-net.org/Webinars/Archive/Rao082012.html

Soft Skills: Your Step-by-Step Guide to Overcome Workplace Challenges to Excel as a Leader by Prof M S Rao (Motivational Press, Inc. 2016)

21 Success Sutras for CEOs by Prof M S Rao (Motivational Press, Inc. April 21, 2016)

Soft Skills Enhancing Employability Connecting Campus with Corporate by Professor M.S.Rao *I K International Publishing House* (August 17, 2010)

Smart Leadership: Lessons for Leaders by M S Rao (Sterling Publishers Pvt Ltd, June 7, 2013)

Success Tools for CEO Coaches by M.S. Rao Shroff Pub & Dist. Pvt. Ltd; First edition (2013)

Leadership CPR: Resuscitating the Workplace Through Civility, Performance and Respect by Ritch K. Eich (Redwood Publishing, LLC, May 7, 2018)

Awesomely Simple: Essential Business Strategies for Turning Ideas Into Action by John Spence (Jossey-Bass; 1 edition, September 8, 2009)

From Smart to Wise: Acting and Leading with Wisdom by Prasad Kaipa and Navi Radjou (John Wiley & Sons 16 April 2013)

Epilogue

"If one is lucky, a solitary fantasy can totally transform one million realities." —Maya Angelou

I have authored this book to achieve gender equality and offer a blueprint to build women leaders as chief executives. If this book helps you excel as a successful leader, it will have done its job. If you put this book down feeling that you are better equipped to excel as an extraordinary leader, I feel that my work as an author has been accomplished.

I would appreciate your valuable feedback to make improvements to this book. You may post your feedback at Facebook Page: https://www.facebook.com/Professor-MS-Rao-451516514937414/ or send me an e-mail: profmsr14@gmail.com. I do keynotes and workshops on learning and leadership. Let me know if you need my services to assist in meeting your individual and organizational goals. I enjoy providing consultation on wellness, leadership mentoring and executive coaching. I encourage you to follow my blogs: http://professormsraovision2030.blogspot.com, http://profmsr.blogspot.com, http://professormsrao.blogspot.com, and http://professormsraoguru.blogspot.com. These blogs pertain to Learning, Leadership, Coaching, Executive Education and Mindfulness. If you find them interesting, please share the links with your friends as knowledge grows when shared.

You may share your thoughts about *Strategies to Build Women Leaders Globally: Think Managers, Think Men; Think Leaders, Think Women* on social media channels including Facebook, Twitter,

LinkedIn, and Google+. I would appreciate a review on your blogs, websites, Amazon or other online bookseller sites.

I sincerely hope that you enjoyed reading this book and found it a useful, practical, and applicable book. If you would like to provide copies to your friends, colleagues or employees, I can offer you bulk discounts with a personalized note and my signature.

Thank you for reading *Strategies to Build Women Leaders Globally: Think Managers, Think Men; Think Leaders, Think Women.* I wish you great happiness and success, both in your business and in your life.

Sincerely,
Professor M.S. Rao, Ph.D
Founder, MSR Leadership Consultants India

ABOUT THE AUTHOR

Professor M.S. Rao, Ph.D
International Leadership Guru
Vision 2030: http://professormsraovision2030.
blogspot.com

Professor M.S. Rao, Ph.D. is an international leadership guru who rose from humble origins. He is recognized as one of the world's leading leadership educators, authors, speakers, coaches, consultants, and practitioners. He is a C-Suite advisor and a sought-after keynote speaker globally. He has thirty-eight years of experience in executive coaching and conducts leadership development training programs for various corporate and educational institutions. He brings a strategic eye and long-range vision given his multifaceted professional experience including military, teaching, training, research, consultancy, and philosophy. He coined a new leadership learning tool—Soft Leadership Grid; a leadership training tool—11E Leadership Grid; and an innovative teaching tool—Meka's Method. His areas of interest include executive coaching, executive education, and leadership. He is passionate about serving and making a difference in the lives of others. He trains a new generation of leaders through leadership education and publications. He advocates gender equality globally (#HeForShe). He shares his leadership wisdom freely with the world on his four blogs. His vision is to build one million students as global leaders by 2030.

He is the Father of 'Soft Leadership' and Founder of MSR Leadership Consultants India. He has authored over forty-five books including the award-winning '21 Success Sutras for CEOs'. His book '21 Success Sutras for Leaders' was selected as a Top 10 Leadership Book of the Year—2013 by San Diego University, USA. He is the recipient of International Coach of the Year 2013 and 'Heart-repreneur® of the Year 2019, USA. He has published more than 250 papers and articles in prestigious international publications including *Leader to Leader, Thunderbird International Business Review, Strategic HR Review, Development and Learning in Organizations, Industrial and Commercial Training, On the Horizon,* and *The Journal of Values-Based Leadership.* He can be reached: profmsr14@gmail.com and additionally maintains four popular blogs including 'Professor M. S. Rao's Vision 2030: One Million Global Leaders' URL: http://professormsraovision2030.blogspot.com.

About The Book

"Can you imagine what the world would be like if women who constitute almost half of the global population had access to education and opportunities and were allowed to contribute their best? We would achieve prosperity globally in all spheres." —Professor M.S. Rao, Ph.D., #HeForShe

This book offers a blueprint to build women CEOs globally. It outlines essential qualities for women CEOs. It explains CEO acumen and offers tools and techniques for women to excel as CEOs. It draws a blueprint for global organizations to build women CEOs. It differentiates between women and men leaders. It illustrates with inspiring examples of women leaders including Melinda Gates, Michelle Obama, Hillary Clinton, Angela Merkel, Indra Nooyi, Ursula Burns, Meg Whitman, and Sheryl Sandberg. It implores women to seize the opportunities to smash through the glass ceiling to excel as CEOs. It unfolds that the companies helmed by women leaders overcame organizational crises successfully. It enlightens that the society cannot grow when one sex is denied with opportunities. It calls upon men to empathize with women and extend their hands with a big heart to groom them as CEOs. It advises women leaders to express their ambition in the early stage of their careers and work hard consistently and relentlessly with a focus and vision to excel as CEOs globally. It advocates gender equality globally. It concludes that when women rise, we all rise.

This book outlines gender, diversity, inclusion, career, coaching, leadership, C-suite and branding. It is a short course on women leadership. You can easily toss the book into a briefcase or purse and read here and there as time allows. It is a quick reference guide for all learners, leaders and those who advocate gender equality globally.

LIST OF BOOKS PUBLISHED
BY THE AUTHOR

1. 21 Success Sutras for CEOs: How Global CEOs Overcome Leadership Challenges in Turbulent Times to Build Good to Great Organizations
2. Secrets of Successful Public Speaking: How to Become a Great Speaker
3. 21 Success Sutras for Leaders
4. Success Tools for CEO Coaches: Be a Learner, Leader and Ladder
5. Smart Leadership: Lessons for Leaders
6. Soft Leadership: Make Others Feel More Important
7. Soft Leadership: An Innovative Leadership Style to Resolve Conflicts Amicably through Soft Skills and Negotiation Skills to Achieve Global Stability, Peace and Prosperity
8. Soft Leadership: Acquire Leadership Ideas and Insights on Visionary, Inspirational and Life Leadership to Stand Out as a Soft Leader Globally
9. Soft Skills: Your Step-by-Step Guide to Overcome Workplace Challenges to Excel as a Leader
10. Soft Skills for Students: Classroom to Corporate
11. Soft Skills: Enhancing Employability
12. Spirit of Indian Youth: Soft Skills for Young Managers
13. Shortlist Your Employer: Acquire Soft Skills to Achieve Your Career and Leadership Success to Excel as a CEO
14. Success Can Be Yours

15. Stand Out! Build a Successful Career and Become a Global Leader
16. Secrets of Your Leadership Success: The 11 Indispensable E's of a Leader
17. Sharpen Your Mind: Acquire Tools to Achieve Your Success
18. Strategies for Improving Your Business Communication: The Book for Leaders to Communicate and Achieve Professional Success
19. Smartness Guide: Success Tools for Students
20. Sage Advice for Students and Educators: Stay Inspired!
21. Soup for Academic Leaders: Acquire Teaching Tools to Achieve Your Academic Leadership Success
22. Spot Your Leadership Style: Build Your Leadership Brand
23. Secrets for Success: Failure is only a Comma, Not a Full Stop
24. Soar Like Eagles! Success Tools for Freshers
25. Student Leaders: Growing From Students To CEOs
26. Success Sutras for Students: Stay Inspired!
27. Striking Stories on Love and Romance: Spread the Message of Love
28. Students: Concerns and Clarifications on Career, Entrepreneurship and Leadership Success
29. Sutras for CEOs: Acquire Leadership Wisdom from Global Leadership Gurus
30. Stay Hungry: Leadership Lessons from Leadership Gurus for Leaders and CEOs
31. Sutras from Management Gurus: Sage Advice for Learners, Leaders and CEOs
32. Stand Out as a Global Leader: Strive for Global Peace and Prosperity to Make a Difference
33. Success Guide: An Inspirational Guide to Excel as a Leader and CEO
34. Sharing Knowledge on Career, Leadership and Success: Improve Your Attitude and Personality to Excel as a Leader
35. Short Stories on Life Leadership: Life is Beautiful!
36. Professor M.S.Rao's Vision 2030: One Million Global Leaders

37. Sharing Leadership Ideas and Insights: Moments and Memories on Indian Educational Institutions through Storytelling
38. Start Leading: Acquire Leadership Lessons from Coaching, Mentoring and Leadership Experts
39. School Leadership: Faculty First, Students Second, And Institutions Third
40. Sharing in Success! A Guide to Acquire Insights on Academic, Career, Leadership and Entrepreneurial Success
41. Success Principles from Management Thinkers: Acquire Leadership Lessons to Create Winning Organization
42. Simplify Your Leadership Strategies: How Great Leaders Build Successful Organizations That Win
43. Spark: The Power to Become Big is Within You!
44. See the Light in You: Acquire Spiritual Powers to Achieve Mindfulness, Wellness, Happiness and Success
45. Strategies to Build Women Leaders Globally: Think Managers, Think Men; Think Leaders, Think Women

MAKING A POSITIVE DIFFERENCE IN THE WORLD

If you have been inspired by *Strategies to Build Women Leaders Globally: Think Managers, Think Men; Think Leaders, Think Women* and want to help women to excel as leaders and C-level executives and help Professor M. S. Rao to advocate gender equality globally, here are some ways you can do that —

- Gift *Strategies to Build Women Leaders Globally* to your friends, family, and colleagues at work.
- Share your thoughts about *Strategies to Build Women Leaders Globally* on Twitter, Facebook, in blogs or write a book review.
- Create a group to work through *Strategies to Build Women Leaders Globally* together, sharing ideas and insights with others.
- If you are responsible for developing people within your organization, you can invest in copies of this book for all your leaders, managers and teams.

www.ingramcontent.com/pod-product-compliance
Lightning Source LLC
Chambersburg PA
CBHW021931190326
41519CB00009B/979